BEING THERE

Being There

New Perspectives on Phenomenology
and the Analysis of Culture

Jonas Frykman & Nils Gilje (eds)

NORDIC ACADEMIC PRESS

Acknowledgments

This book would never have been written without the generosity of different research councils and foundations. The research project 'Annerledeslandet' with the Norwegian Research Council (NFR) contributed financially to much field-work and made possible the conference in Dubrovnik, as did the Faculty of Philosophy at Bergen University. The Centre for European Studies at Lund University has participated in financing fieldwork for some of the participants through the project 'Borders of Europe'. Sigfrid Svensson's Foundation at the Department of European Ethnology at Lund University has made translations of the non-English papers possible. The Introduction, Jonas Frykman's and Kjell Hansen's texts were translated by Sue Glover, Word-Stugan i Rimbo HB. As editors we are deeply indebted to the valuable comments by our colleagues Orvar Löfgren, Lund; Billy Ehn, Umeå; Torunn Selberg, Bergen, and Lena Gerholm Stockholm. Special thanks go to the many students and scholars at different levels at the universities in Bergen and in Lund who have so actively taken part in discussing the perspectives of phenomenology within contemporary ethnology.

Nordic Academic Press
Box 1206
s-221 05 Lund, Sweden
Tel: +46 46 33 34 50
Fax: +46 46 18 96 85
E-mail: info@nordicacademicpress.com
www.nordicacademicpress.com

Contents

JONAS FRYKMAN & NILS GILJE

Being There

An Introduction

I would say that there has been too much talk about phenomenology, and not enough phenomenological work. One does not
always have to insist that what one is doing is phenomenology,
but one ought to work phenomenologically, that is, descriptively,
creatively – intuitively, and in a concretizing manner. Instead of
simply applying concepts to all sorts of things, concepts ought to
come forward in movements of thoughts springing from the spirit
of language and the power of intuition.[1]

Hans-Georg Gadamer

Doing Phenomenology

A certain place connects the contributors to this book – a unique
material and social environment. A weeklong workshop was held
at the Inter University Centre in Dubrovnik at the beginning of
October 2001.[2] A small group of philosophers, political scientists,
anthropologists and ethnologists from Norway, Sweden, Croatia,
Australia and New Zealand respectively had made their way to
that remarkable city in the heat of late summer to discuss some
of the practical connections between philosophical traditions and
contemporary analysis of culture. Such interchanges are always
hazardous. So many pitfalls open up when you take the step from
the theoretical, well-reasoned position that philosophy can offer,
and confront it with a more difficult to grasp everyday reality. Those
who tread the boundaries can easily come under attack. But the
potential benefit of the enterprise sometimes outweighs the risks.
Today there is a yearning to be once again inspired by a system-

atic approach, since the ways of analysing culture seem so diverse and lead in many different directions. Is there any kind of 'post constructivist' perspective and a revitalisation in relation to theory and method? What possibilities are there to sharpen the tools for further field research within ethnology? A certain hesitation towards ethnological spadework follows when directions are unclear. An inclination towards the study and the library sometimes indicates such an uncertainty about the core of the discipline.

This longing increases when a growing number of researchers find themselves provoked by disquieting questions concerning transnationalism and the multicultural, xenophobia, the use of violence and similar attempts to homogenise people's cultural identity. What effective investigative instruments are available to the field researcher then? As Michael Jackson said in his opening lecture, 'Philosophy has always been good at asking questions, but cultural and behavioural scientists are then called upon to come up with interesting answers.' This book therefore tries to illustrate the importance of detailed field studies from a phenomenological point of departure by giving practical examples.

In some ways phenomenology is almost taken for granted within contemporary ethnology in the Nordic countries although, if we may say so, more as a justification for doing studies of 'everyday life' than as a systematic approach. One can only speculate about the reasons for this. The aspirations of the empirical cultural scientists to concretely 'do phenomenology' have often failed because the actual translation work from the philosophical tradition was too demanding. Researchers progressed to different kinds of adaptations and patchworks where inspiration was visible but entire perspectives were missing. Thus studies have been enlightened by phenomenology, but with different degrees of clarity. Many ethnologists interested in that – alternative – scientific tradition have run up against the seemingly irrelevant questions of what the differences were between Edmund Husserl, Martin Heidegger, Alfred Schutz, Maurice Merleau-Ponty and Jean Paul Sartre – and in the process have missed the excitement. How they stood in relation to each other is sometimes less important than seeing what they have in common. The issue then easily tends to become a jigsaw puzzle or yet another instance of *l'art pour l'art*. The route has looked promising, but it has been difficult to turn the insights into concrete analyses. Perhaps it is more like a way of thinking rather than a method for analysing everyday cultural patterns? It has also teetered on the brink of appearing trivial: does it say more than the obvious, albeit in a much more impenetrable way?

Phenomenology's constant invitation to 'go to things as they are' seems just like the *vademecum* that every ethnographer ought to bring along to the field. Why then has it been so difficult to make it simple? Against this backdrop, the purpose of the seminar was to discuss how one converts this philosophical direction into practical analyses.

And why not? The wish to renew science by doing field research probably mirrors both processes within the scientific world *and* the social experience that people are having in contemporary society. In the last decade, the principal line of enquiry within ethnology has been to deal with cultural identities: nation, gender, age, class, ethnicity and place. Identity is what people are supposed to have, but also what they are building in some kind of bricolage as an individual response to the demands of a complex society. Many scholars have picked up on typical situations where such identities are defined and many have analysed the discourses – texts, instructions and narratives – where identities have been shaped. Gradually a very comprehensive and sophisticated humanistic and cultural scientific discussion about identity-construction has developed. However there has been very little about the actions, the practice and the environment in which identities functions. Formations of identities are better known than identities that are lived. How the subject creates and experiences identity and how it resists the attempt to be influenced is a field yet to be explored. While much wisdom has been devoted to how identities are constructed, surprisingly little attention is paid to how this is experienced from within – and what 'within' really means.

People in complex societies are actors that must find paths to walk. They are forced into a spectrum of individual solutions – both in space (different places) and in time (changing with phases in the lifecycle). And they are used to being noticed due to their identities.

9

They are brought up to be consumers, with the special liberties and restrictions that this carries. Both the market and the political system should pay attention to their demands. External pressure forces them into continuous and new combinations, approximate interpretations and creative misunderstandings. The rich array of images, symbols and discourses that people must choose from becomes – like the meals on our table – increasingly varied and alluring and thus harder to avoid. As with individuals, national cultures also become varied in general terms: the social-security system, the labour market, the outer organisation of lifecycles and residential patterns.

In order to orientate themselves in this world, people need open access to all their faculties, the capacity to use all their senses as well as judgement and knowledge. In other words, there is obviously a great demand for theories that can clarify how individuals function as active culture builders as well as being actors in an existence where possible identities simultaneously become the result of their *actions* as well as mental, reflexive construction projects. How do they shape something of their own from the reality that surrounds them? How can they in turn play upon the environment and make it *happen*? The answer to such questions lies not only in how identities are constructed, but also in how they are lived.

Of course, in that position the demand for theories that can put both words and concepts to that complex and mutual exchange between people and their surrounding cultural and natural *environment* grows. In the new phenomenology that is now on offer, it becomes obvious that subjectivity and materiality are not mutually exclusive, but rather presuppose each other. Or to put it another way: talking about the subject's materiality and the material's subjectivity.

The notion of the intertwining of identity and the environment in which people engage as actors is central in this discussion. For the researcher it could very well be rooted in the conviction that science and art are quite closely related. The scholar is no longer an objective observer that stands at the side of his or her object of study and registers the course of events. Instead he or she is a participant and should as such use imagination and intuition, allowing themselves to be inspired and implicated by the specific situation. Scholars are not seeking *nomothetic* knowledge – generalisations – but to describe the specific that is deeply experienced and is therefore universal. So far the quest for knowledge is in a fundamental way *idiographic*. The researcher seeks the unique and by the same token what is deeply communal in the singular.

Naturally, such ideas point in the direction of an ecological awareness, since they indicate that identity is worked out in relation to an existing environment, to objects and to places – although that is not dealt with to any great extent in this collection of essays. The existing context is the very fabric where patterns take shape and actions are carried out. In other words, each situation is like a window of opportunity. Such ideas need not be rooted in the multinational society, but that could very well be the case. They will explain how identities are formed in relation to the surrounding human environment and fields of concrete action. Identities are not at first hand a question of ideas but of ordinary practice – the tactile, sensual and practical relationship to the natural and humanly created environment.

The anthropologist Bradd Shore points out (1996) that there is a certain risk that people's dependency on their social and material environment is restricted – if they merely see the world as a social and cultural construction. It appears as imperfect if it is determined at people's discretion – if one sees it as a result of the image or 'worldview' one makes of the world – putting quotation marks round what there is. Martin Heidegger called the aspirations to make the world into an image – something completely humanly created – *Bestellen* or enframing. The risk implied by this was to give the green light to exploitation. One sees the environment as if it was 'standing-reserve,' like a single, large petrol station ready for human use. Pay and fill up! As yet this is only one of the market segments! Its value is determined by what one is able to get out of it. 'Human beings are "human resources". Books and works of art become "information resources" and writing becomes "word-processing", as if language was also just a resource to be manipulated. Time itself has become standing-reserve: well illustrated by software tycoon Bill Gates' pronouncement, "Just in terms of allocation of time resources, religion is not very efficient".' (Polt 1999:171, cf Heidegger 1977).

On the other hand you are exposed to the risk of stopping to be attentive to the fact that the world is so much bigger than you can ever imagine. Modern information technology has stretched the user to formless proportions. Shore asks what happens to the person that all the time looks at the world as if it was not there – reducing it to a human construction. For instance, the idea that the world really could be captured through computer screens or cyber space does not make it any clearer, but rather quite the opposite – more obscure. It puts the individual firmly in the centre so that what is familiar is dimmed. The neighbourhood becomes a projection screen for the will and for language, but at the same time is itself invisible. That was what Heidegger alluded to when he spoke about how an increasingly technological view of the world leads the individual into a virtual world in the worst-sense. 'It darkens. Losing something of the poetic "indwelling", which should mark what Heidegger likes to call the "coming into being with the world"' (Shore 1996:144). However, as it might easily appear from Heidegger, that gloom is not a process restricted to an epoch but something that constantly accompanies high technological society like a shadow and demands that individuals and groups inform themselves about it and take a stand (cf Lash 1999). If his statements should be taken in the literary sense Heidegger would shudder in fear at the presence of fax machines, cellular phones and the Internet (Polt 1999:60). But that would be to reduce a complex reasoning into a simplistic critique of technology.

So perhaps the interest in phenomenology is one of many signs of a seeking for theories that make a mental note of how people make use of culture and the environment, technology as well as art.

Being There

The discussions during the seminar in Dubrovnik were of course directed towards theme, theory and method. But in the afternoons when the sun hung low in the sky and it was too warm to sit indoors at the Inter University Centre, we went down to the beach with towels slung over our shoulders. The asphalted stub of road gradually became a rough track that led us over the rocks, past the park of pine trees, past the wall surrounding the warm grey coloured monastery outlined against the shimmering blue bay. A bell tinkled the time for prayer and the waves pulsed in protracted sweeps against the rocks. Children laughed loudly and scantily dressed youngsters moved away when we came in sight. There was freshness beside the water and time to let the thoughts sink in. Re-flections about the discursive in culture, worldviews, and that which was humanly created melted away for a moment. The bay was here long before we came. Ever since the days when the Argonauts had searched for that golden fleece, ships from the Greek archipelago had sailed on that very horizon where oil tankers on their way to Rijeka were now outlined. It was here that galleys from Rome and Venice had collected their goods and procured new slaves. Sailors from the independent city state of Dubrovnik-Ragusa must also have observed the walled city, situated on the small strip of land below the mountain, with the same wonder as visitors from more recent times.

And the academic discussions about dwelling and opening yourself to that which is already there, that which is also partly humanly created – but only partly – had a naturalness about them when we sensually turned our pale autumn bodies towards the late summer sun. The challenges from the seminar room to enrich the analysis of discourses with sensual experiences and action, with emplaced and embodied subjectivity, became easy to understand with the smell of the sea that met our nostrils, with the sight of water hammered in silver that dissolved in the heat haze, by the taste of salt in the air and in the noise of the wind. Of course there was experience before the word, and certainly there is a living imagination that inhabits the world around us with ideas and reveries long before it has been theorised and shaped into ready packaged analyses and interpretations! In other words, you actually discover the sense of bathing by just doing it.

Blessed by the open atmosphere, which is often created when you are far away from home and you come closer to each other, something also happened in the meeting between researchers; between the different places that we were told about and the very locality where we were. The complicated became so very simple and this shines through in many of the essays. It is really about the perspective that the researchers bring forward, just as the idea that lies in the verbal perspectives – a way of observing the coupling by doing justice to experience and that which is going on in people's day-to-day life.

Practically Speaking

All the authors of this book are seeking a new and vital starting point when it comes to describing identities – and in its extension, man in relation to culture. After post-modernism, the deconstructions in post-structuralism, and the linguistic and semiotic turn within the cultural sciences, there is an understandable curiosity in people as *experiencers* rather than as *receivers* of different kinds of messages, as *creators of meaning* rather than *interpreters* and as *actors* rather than *observers*. There is also an intention to go to things as they are and to the places in order to see how nature and the material influence people's ideas and actions much more than what they themselves are able to project into them.

From a cultural point of view, that which can seem seductive within phenomenology is the intention to constantly pay attention to practice. Of course, all the identities are in some respect 'constructed', formed from the equipment there is to use and what there is in the moment of experience. But does that mean that they become less filled with meaning if the researcher manages to point out how they are 'fitted together'? Identities are not containers that are possible to fill with content, but an 'opening' – a way of coming closer to the surroundings where your own experience all the time forms starting points. There is always someone there, able to experience.

The father of modern phenomenology, Edmund Husserl, says that focussing on experience is about 'being there'. This implies that phenomenology is occupied with describing things as they appear to the consciousness. 'In other words, the way problems, things, and events are approached must involve *taking their manner of appearance to consciousness into consideration*' (Moran 2000:6). You must therefore take both the experiencer and the surrounding world – 'mankind, animals and the whole of creation' – very seriously indeed. Here it should be noted that the English language does not differentiate between 'lived experience' as in the German word *Erlebnis*, or the Swedish *upplevelse* and the already elapsed experience that is the object of analytical or abstract knowledge, as in the German *Erfahrung* and the Swedish *erfarenhet* (cf Casey 1996:18).

By going to the experiencer (*upplevaren*), by making *experience* the starting point, it becomes possible to see how, in the moment of interpretation, people do not just lend their inspiration to the surroundings but rather *bring them to life* and let them *happen*. In that process, new combinations and new constructions are made all the time. These are both individual and collective processes. Here phenomenology offers an analytical path by focussing on the consequences of actions rather than their causes, writes the Italian sociologist and psychotherapist Alberto Melucci. Phenomenology is a theory that concentrates on how experiences are set out in action, 'how people act and how they can change their life if they so wish. It is a process oriented approach that, unlike psychoanalysis, is less determined by the *contents* of experience, especially from the past' (Melucci 1992:188).

It is quite possible that the attractive force of phenomenology is merely an expression of science's insatiable appetite for new approaches. Every discipline has its own generations, its own strain of practised manipulations and explanations. One has to repeatedly redefine concepts in order to articulate contemporary impressions. While the study of experienced (*upplevda*) worlds becomes important in today's ethnology, it is perhaps about a renewed belief in the credibility of the empirical. Of course it can also be about ethnology's recurrent striving to take 'the perspective from below' from the situated position of the very individual that experiences. This aspiration has been a strong – more or less visible – undercurrent in Nordic ethnology since the 1970's – and visible to a greater or lesser extent. It was often expressed in the quest for conducting empirical field-studies.

There is an attractive empirical stability in 'situated praxis' – based on what people do in actual situations – which invites fieldwork, collection of data and new discoveries. Such a freshly produced knowledge makes it possible to criticise adopted truths and established dogmas. In times of unrest a longing for something 'authentic and genuine' is always created – something that can give a foothold in a world of floating signs and symbols. What is therefore more natural than to go to the experiencer – to the body, the senses, and the everyday life-world with its people, things and places?

Ethnographic Variety

The essays in this book are therefore about the relationships of people, things and places just as they are experienced and created. They certainly point in many geographical directions. We don't only meet an indignant newspaper reader in Sydney, as in the anthropologist Ghassan Hage's essay of the Lebanese in Diaspora, and it isn't only multicultural contexts that are on the agenda in Maja Povrzanovic Frykman's or Francine Lorimer's papers. In fact it is the application and the method's usefulness that is illustrated in the different essays. Consequently the reader is also able, as in Kirsti Mathiesen Hjemdahl's contribution, to accompany happy scampering Norwegian children on a visit to Moomin Valley in Finland. For them this is a wonderland, while their adult companions yawn at the prospect of yet another theme park. The events that little Aksel encountered consisted of stories, flights of imagination and what the senses revealed in just that moment – and the excitement of sitting next to a soft troll that slowly whispers, 'Moomin loves you'! That impression was not there waiting for him in the park and it was not planned by the adults, but sprang from the actual encounter.

Then, in Francine Lorimer's description, we are allowed to take part in the midsummer celebrations in Copenhagen, where it is the custom to burn dolls that symbolise witches; a good old Danish tradition that is repeated in similar form every year. But is it really the dolls that go up in smoke? From that predictable Nordic custom we have, in one giddy moment, learned how children, in their imaginations, step from the everyday into the imaginary. Is it that which is unfamiliar, undesirable or foreign whirling around in the air that these children from another background are sensing? That world which is theirs vanishes in the direction of their gaze and in the shower of sparks. When the well-integrated and friendly Nordic cultures are seen from a transnational perspective, dimensions other than the sweet and friendly appear.

Michael Jackson confronts us with Western metaphysics and rationality when he allows us to meet a mother in Sierra Leone. During the horrors of civil war, she happened to find herself in the wrong place at the wrong time and had her hand chopped off. Bleeding, the mother Kamara fled from her home village with her little daughter – also disfigured in the same way. How can you become reconciled with the perpetrator and abstain from taking revenge is the question. How do you maintain your humanity and avoid becoming a victim and turning the perpetrator into an executioner? To answer that question you can, like Jackson, go into another culture's subjectivity and apply double hermeneutics. Kamara was in the wrong place but the perpetrators were not out to get her – it was not her *identity* that was offensive to them.

This situation made her realise the boundaries of her freedom and patterns of behaviour. But for the western relief workers, who thought of human rights in abstract terms, it was difficult to see her in her context or understand life from her perspective. It was only by making an effort for the *person* that, according to them, brotherly feeling could be defended. And that is why Kamara now lives in a camp for amputees. Her daughter has gone to the USA to get a new prosthesis. Both have been deprived of the relationship to each other, to the place, to the hometown where one can live with dignity intact. Meaning is created between people, in the place and from the life they have to live. At first hand it is intersubjective and not intrapsychic. What she and others like her needed most was help that could enable them to resume a normal life; things that protected them, education for the children, medicine to heal the wounds and so on. Only a mending of the immediate world could create continuity in life.

On a coach journey between Malmö and Zagreb, Maja Povrzanovic Frykman tells us about identities being something that springs from actions and practice. In physical terms she shows what it means to be a traveller that can afford only a bus ticket – like millions of guest workers within Europe. What does it feel like to first of all have your identity reduced to that of traveller and compatriot, then via passport control and border crossings be defined as unwelcome and a second class European citizen? These are experiences that hardly come out in verbal statements but must be tangibly experienced in all their bodily manifestations. Meaning is revealed as a stressful bodily reality. She raises the crucial question about how cultural identity is something that is constantly negotiated in practical situations, something that has as much a physical as a conceptual dimension. 'The cognitive approach reflected in 'believing' and 'imagining' communities has to be combined with the phenomenological approach of bodily 'feeling', bridging the gap between discourse and body'.

From the steps of the National Museum in Budapest, Kjell Hansen talks about the overall difficulties of using yourself as the experiencer. The fieldworker is reduced to a stereotype, made into an outsider that neither understands the language, the rituals nor the reason for the jollity. What do you do when you lack knowledge of the history and discourse but are exposed to your other 'sensory impulses'? It is striking what a wealth of information floods in just by participating in the actions, demonstrations and celebrations. But this meant that his fieldwork became not very well-grounded 'participant observation', which puts a considerable distance between the scientific thoughtful observer – but 'shared experience' where he followed the participants' visual direction and took part in their actions. He shows the importance of the fieldworker 'being there' – body and soul.

In the study of regionalism in Istria, Croatia, Jonas Frykman formulates the question about sensually experiencing a place, a landscape and a region. What flights of imagination does that give rise to and what are the impressions of the world that capture us and which can only vaguely be put into words? What happened when the adopted history of the place is only one of many components in the ability to experience? In order to see Istria with new eyes, a poetic renewal of language and use of metaphor are called for. After the collapse of Communism, the region opened up to the West and now a cultural reframing of something that before was quite forgotten is taking place. As well as the local inhabitants, tourism moves towards descriptions that deal with the body, the senses, feelings and experiences. In addition, the subjective world is found in the new economy – the experience, *Erlebnis* – in focus as the producer of authenticity and genuineness.

Looking Back

To seek new inspiration from different forms of phenomenological methods is to follow a well-beaten Nordic ethnological track. The mere aspiration of starting with the everyday, to see 'culture from below' and to take the perspective of 'the other' or 'thinking with one's feet' is in itself an obvious effort to want to understand culture in use. In this respect a kind of phenomenological approach has been integrated with science – especially in Sweden – ever since it started to work systematically with what has been coined as *kulturanalys* or the analysis of culture in the 1970's. Yes, perhaps even more so then because there was a strong emphasis on ethnographic fieldwork in the 70's research. It gave new insights to the description of life as culture – whether in suburban society, day care centres, fishing villages or any place at the side of the road. It was like discovering your own very parochial society, which had not yet ended up in the cultural press or on the pages of history books.

When the concept of *kulturanalys* – analysis of culture – of the 70's and 80's became successful, tools and concepts that could capture what was seen in a single formula were simultaneously looked for. Something that could make patterns from 19th-Century peasant society, of the victorious bourgeoisie at the turn of the century and the emerging working class at the beginning of the 20th Century, comparable with other worlds or other cultures. Concepts and operations were needed to make the domestic more exotic and put it at an arm's-length analytical distance. Previous investigations within ethnology had either been chronological or spatial. Before the 70's it was even more rare to describe the communities or artefacts in terms of 'culture'.

In order to find answers to the question about how the Swedish experience compared with the British, American, or Australian, perspectives were needed that demonstrated recognisable structures and patterns. They were available via the contemporary Anglo-Saxon traditions within anthropology, such as empirical British structuralism and the study of symbols by such prominent scholars as Edmund Leach, Victor Turner and Mary Douglas – and American cognitive anthropology and ethno-methodology where J.P. Spradley and C.O. Frake had the greatest influence. French structuralism in the Claude Levi-Straussian tradition never really made it into the Scandinavian ethnological scene. Therefore structural Marxism of the time did not have any significant influence while the more empiric studies of E.P. Thompson where he asked how class *happened* – not what it *was* – became quite influential. Another tradition was the study of historical socialisation processes like those that appeared in the German *Kapital-logik*, with names like Klaus Ottomeyer, Alfred Krovoza and Thomas Ziehe. When the influence came from phenomenology, it was via the English classic, Berger & Luckman's *The Social Construction of Reality* of 1966. However, it was mostly understood as a pretext for the legitimacy of a kind of ethno-methodology, focussing on the meaning of everyday life as an analytical space. What was missing in that important book, however, was a really thorough discussion of culture, and their writings therefore had a limited impact on what was then significant: method, and the *doing* of ethnography.

Within this development of ethnological analysis of culture there was, in part, an enormous enthusiasm about the possibility of translating the more general theoretical argument of anthropology to the domestic level. There was so much to describe! But at the same time there was a limitation built into the perspective because culture came to appear as something cognitive rather than social and action based. There was a tendency to provide the researcher with 'non-intuitive procedures' in order to discover people's classification system (Hastrup et al. 1975:190). That mentalist emphasis never disappeared and actually became strengthened when theories about modernity were integrated with the analysis of culture in the 1990's. The conscious building of identity was looked upon as a mainly intellectually driven project. During the 90's, Anthony Giddens and Ulrich Beck became the distinct inspirers of this line of thought.

The first more systematic attempt to apply phenomenological perspectives within Scandinavian ethnology came through the work of Lena Gerholm in Stockholm and Mats Lindqvist and Beatriz Lindqvist in Lund. It signified a departure from that Anglo-Saxon inspiration and those researchers now linked up with continental – German and French – philosophy. Perhaps this was most clearly carried out in Lena Gerholm's dissertation, 'Project Culture and Culture Project' (1986). Here theories from Edmund Husserl and Alfred Schutz were used and practiced. Gerholm described how the Swedish National Council for Culture wanted to make life more 'meaningful' and 'rich' for citizens that were marginalized in different ways in society in general and in their housing areas in particular. A project was therefore launched that should satisfy their cultural needs. People that didn't take part in that general cultural amenity ran the risk of facing deserted and empty lives, it was believed. But the planners' idea of what high culture was and its function as a remedy to increase the quality actually concealed people's culture and everyday creativity from them. Not even state sponsored high culture exists independently of the people that use it. In Lena Gerholm's study it was made obvious how the abstract rationality of the planners created an entirely separate world in the supposedly impoverished suburbs. People related to each other, and to objects and activities in manifold ways. The concept of life-world was launched for the first time in Sweden and was used as an instrument for ethnographic investigation.

Both Mats Lindqvist (1987) and Beatriz Lindqvist (1991) were first inspired by the Czech praxis-theorist, Karel Kosík, who more explicitly – and from a Marxist point of view – analysed how culture was based in action. Beatriz Lindqvist showed how Swedes and refugees that came from South America met over things and activities. For working class people, the material world could work as an effective bridge between groups. Intellectual revolutionaries that had limited possibilities of working together with their new countrymen met difficulties in the search for 'a common ground' by which they could be integrated. To them everyday experiences were constantly sifted through a tight ideological filter.

For a long time these works seemed to be quite unique examples

within Scandinavian ethnology as consistently accomplished phenomenological analyses. It is thought provoking to reflect on their
limited impact. They were not actually setting fashion in the same
way as the increasingly sophisticated and elaborated *kulturanalys*
– analysis of culture. It might be that the concept of *culture* with its
rich connotations of signs, symbols, rituals and interpretations was
too undeveloped in this line of thought. The other tradition had such
an alluring practical dimension, a do-ability that made it convincing
without really having to argue for it. First you demarcate a 'culture'
and then you make an analysis of it. In reality it presupposes that
there is an object – something that can be analysed. The methods
inspired from phenomenology were certainly thought provoking,
but how do you *do* them?

Being Re-inspired

It wasn't until the late 1990's that the interest in referring back to
phenomenology was again launched in the Scandinavian world
of ethnology. In 1997, the Danish historian of ideas, Niels Kayser
Nielsen, wrote an essay on a classic ethnological subject – namely,
national identity. With the help of, among others, the American
geographer Yi-Fu Tuan, he could discuss national identity not as
an ideology or interpellation, nor as culture or individually shaped
habitus, not as rituals or symbols – but as one of many practical
ways of orienting oneself in relation to the surrounding landscape.
Not 'by virtue of the tasks one has to do here and not so much by
virtue of a mental sense of belonging, that is to an idea or principle'
(Nielsen 1997:85). For the first time the landscape was integrated as
something other than a projection or an essence. It was something
that actively contributed to the shaping of practice and the production of national self-understanding.

Scandinavian identities cannot be analysed as result of an idea,
a principle, or taught knowledge – because they are things that
happen, that take place in people's interactions with each other
and with the landscape. The specific place that is fashioned when
people take possession of the landscape, through walks, skiing or
mushroom picking, also activates the material – the landscape and

nature. Certainly nature is created by culture, but culture in an intricate way becomes created by nature through these exercises. It can be 'determined by experience, thus becoming a knowledge of what is shared in a practical tradition of knowledge, which is not "pure" or principled but is rather a continuation of various types of tasks. This is a living and lived experience which has the character of relations between people bound in a certain practical context' (Nielsen 1997:86). Here Nielsen expressed something that was quite obvious in the existing practice of contemporary research and linked it to a comprehensive level of explanation.

Since then a wide variety of studies has developed that illustrates the productiveness of making this translation. Ideas are reaching maturity by being tried out in applied research. For instance, in a dissertation Elisabeth Berglin (2000) described a peasant painter of the 18th Century. Like all folk-artists, Johannes Nilsson in Breared was of course stereotyped in his expression. He could quite easily be analysed from the point of view of his style, from traditional motifs and colours. But Berglin concentrated on how an entire peasant world was articulated on his wall hangings and how his native district, with its landscape and people, was his true source of inspiration. The neighbourhood he lived in became visible in another way. The connection between the wall hangings and the context in which they were created was a more rewarding way of describing than mere motif-analysis and attributing existing paintings.

At the University of Bergen, Heidi Richardson (2000) presented a thesis in which she investigated Norwegian 'green-movement farmers'. A lot has been written about that issue in the field of the theory of modernity. This has rather been seen as a response to the disintegration of fixed affiliations, a compensatory longing for making whole that which society has divided; a sign or a symptom of what happens in a globalised world. But that approach became too intellectual – too abstract because they had chosen life rather than protest. Richardson did not focus on the *reasons* for the green-movementers' decision to pull from the city out to the country in a kind of protest against environmental pollution and global capitalism. Instead she focussed on the *consequences* of their decision. What did it lead to? What were the results in their own life-world and how did their ecological way of living have repercussions on the Norwegian cultural environment and agricultural policy? Taking agency seriously and looking at the consequences of actions rather than at their possible causes became a leading theme for many other studies from the same department.

In her investigation of contemporary environmental concern, Connie Reksten-Kapstad (2002), resolutely distanced herself from the term *kulturanalys,* cultural analysis. She suggested that there was actually more of a hidden theory in the method than was usually recognised. The flexible searchlight of analysis, looking for unexpected combinations and choosing information from all kinds of different places, offered many openings, but at the same time made permanent the notion that culture was a construction of the mind. 'By interpreting culture as text it was above all possible to put together different categories of sources and analyse them under one hat' (Reksten-Kapstad 2002:25).

When studying politics she wanted to look at the doing, at activities and an analysis of culture inspired by language-based theories pointed in the wrong direction. All the young people that protested against the Norwegian so called 'gas production issue' – the expansion of gas power plants that would further increase the nation's emission of poisonous carbon dioxide – were concentrated on action. How would you be able to understand action as action and not as text, symbol or representations of something else? That was her recurring question. And for that question the text-oriented analysis did not provide any real answers. Even if it claims that it includes the concepts 'experience' and 'context' it would break its own boundaries if it really went beyond the 'linguistic inspira-tion'. Instead Reksten-Kapstad went to what the young people really intended and did – to place, body, experience and reactions. Committing themselves to the social movement against gas power meant that they embarked upon something that they intended to change and which in turn came to change them and their lives. They could not be understood as 'passive actors that rest in an al-ready established meaning and in already decided definitions' (2002: 167). The very place where they gathered to demonstrate – which was the site where a gas plant was supposed to be built – became culturally generative. Together with the things they surrounded themselves with – banners, tents, dresses and instruments – the place itself became an actor. Furthermore, the environment itself, the contaminated environment, became an agent through being articulated. How do you make gas visible if not through things, place and people? The environment was therefore not a resource to exploit and manipulate for economic gains, but a whole world in which people lived and breathed. To say that it was a cultural construction appeared scornful when the release of carbon dioxide could actually be measured in an increasing percentage.

In her doctoral thesis on Norwegian theme parks, Kirsti Mathiesen Hjemdahl (2002) opposes the line of researchers that chose to interpret this Disneyland-like phenomenon as mere text or a completed universe of meaning. Where is the Kodak Picture-Point, and where are the paper-strip paths you should follow in order to have the already programmed experiences? Of course the cultural critique of the 'theme parking of culture' had its justification. There the world was really transformed to a text and an ironical programming of authenticity. But at the same time the critique too easily went in for a genre that smelled of the well-known words 'disorder', 'decay' and 'commercialisation', of everything that is solid melting into thin air (Berman 1987). If you look at culture from the decay hypothesis angle it readily stands out as a thing. Not even a theme park is a system of signs that can be read with the answer book in your hand when it is used. Even the most clever marketing can only explain part of its popularity.

Instead of seeing what a theme park in some respect *is* she instead chose to study how it *happens*. What was it that enticed a little child, over and over again, to run through false fronted houses and caress the Moomin-troll dolls with zips in their backs? What world of possibilities presented themselves to a boy that suddenly held a pirate's sword in his hand? An exciting fencing match with the parking meter seemingly transforms it from being a dead thing into an adversary to destroy. Falling leaves were like darts that rained from the air. The sword worked like Martin Heidegger's famous hammer – it makes one discover that the world is full of nails and therefore susceptible to blows.

The unambiguous in the culture is generally something that you can gradually learn. And in that process the academics are especially active with their analyses. But what happened to imagination; the undefineability that turns the environment into a space in which a boy can *act*?

In the book *Fönster mot Europa* (Window towards Europe), the editors Kjell Hansen and Karin Salomonsson (2001) emphatically pleaded with researchers in Lund for greater reference to the material culture, places and things. It is through these that people develop their identities. The relationship is concealed in today's enthusiasm for discussing what a European identity could be. Building Europe from above seems much more likely to be the issue than seeing these processes from below. Remarkably, the formation of the European space very much seems to add to the importance of sensual experiences, of places and things. The interest in cultural heritage and genealogy brings the local in parallel with the global or European to the fore. 'We understand, approach and act in relation to the world from cultural categories. But it is the participation in the world that not only gives us knowledge about it but also the cultural categories' (2001:16). It is in the close reality that the abstract is rendered meaning and content, and 'concepts like history, nation, region, ethnicity or Europe are constantly reworked and renegotiated in order to create something viable in everyday life' (Frykman & Niedermüller 2002:4).

Throughout this book, ethnologists are discussing how things and places take on the role of becoming actors and subjects. Regions are not so much about roots and belonging where people are under the influence of pre-given rules, as 'entrances to beehives buzzing with images – information, interpretations of smells and tastes, and directions of the surrounding world' (Frykman 2002: 65). Every articulation of roots and affiliation to place has the potential of leading 'to a redefinition of places and of material culture'. Cultural heritage could not simply be looked upon as a reaction to modernisation or globalisation, but a search for new rules, 'a kind of mobile monument which makes up a reservoir of the past that can bring political power to the fore' (Hansen 2002: 31). As Eva Reme illustrates in her study of the European City of Culture in the year 2000, Bergen, the past brought to the fore as cultural heritage filled the present with rather unspecified 'memory places ... that ... constitute a potential storage room for various small and anonymous events as well as those we celebrate officially and recognise as our collective memory' (Reme 2002:45). Such possibility of creating a kind of 'personal heritage' is most clearly visible in the upsurge of regional and local food specialties. The phenomenon of 'Slow Food' is an illustration of how the local is 'produced, reproduced and reshaped on an everyday level' in a very personal way (Burstedt 2002:154).

This reshaping of places through action is most extensively elaborated in an essay on the siege of Dubrovnik. Under the repeated shelling from the mountains above the city, people became aware of how intimately their lives were dependent upon the material world, upon the natural environment and upon other people. Is identity something you build and construct as a reflexive project? Or is it something you become aware of in certain places under certain conditions? In extreme moments the limitations of this free-floating mentalist approach become apparent: 'The animals and the people were living beings inhabiting the same place defined by violence. In a very basic way they were all sharing the same destiny: they were all exposed to the same shelling' (Povrzanovic Frykman 2002: 84). What give places their specificity is not only events casually experienced by people living there and freely interacting with one another. In this case violence is making them *happen*.[2]

The impact of recent years' research registers a trend that exists in time. They indicate how rewarding it has become to begin this rendering of the philosophical traditions to concrete analyses of culture. What is already present as a well-established intellectual tradition of such cultural analysis, *kulturanalys,* seems to gain a lot from this new expansion into new perspectives.

Being Implicated

Ghassan Hage portrays his countryman, Maurice, as sitting in his dry cleaners shop in Sydney. He keeps an example of 'his' newspaper from the homeland under the counter and reads it between customers. He grumbles about Lebanon's politicians. He strikes the paper with his hand, scolds and argues. It isn't the text he reads that upsets him. It is the Prime Minister himself that he is after. With its many news items, advertisements, pictures and articles, the newspaper is much more than just a piece of information about Lebanon. In that moment it *is* Lebanon and he is home again – in body and soul, sadness and joy. That the Prime Minister is intending to travel to villainous Syria is a slap in Maurice's face! As a reader he is simultaneously a child and a young man, among relatives and friends, on the streets of Beirut and present in that dazzling bright Mediterranean landscape. That world is in him as strongly as the newly washed clothes that surround him in the shop. 'If I was in Lebanon, I would spit on them one by one!' he emphasises so as to convince Hage that the reality there is a world where he belongs. He doesn't need to return in order to be there – it's enough that the newspaper brings that presence to life. 'Think only what it means to go back to a place you know, finding it full of memories and expectations, old things and new things, the familiar and the strange, and much more besides', writes the philosopher Edward Casey in his discussion of how places have a capacity to hold memories (1996:24).

People who think of their homeland far away easily see it as a living being. Reading the homeland's newspaper is like talking to someone you know. And as in every personal relation you claim a real commitment from the counterpart, for presence and authenticity. Thus the information is not in the text, but the text is the introductory handshake that affirms that the conversation can begin.

The researcher is using this example to enter the discussion about what it means to be 'implicated', or participatory. And he makes us question what actually happens in the meeting between the reader and the physical presence of the newspaper from home. What are the circumstances in which both thing and text can be the starting point for imagination, insights and memories? How do both thing and text achieve that obvious closeness and the feelings that you yourself can experience when you visit your home or an environment that you are familiar with? The word 'belong' signifies something that develops over a long period of time and in close proximity to things and people. An ever-so-friendly invitation from a foreigner to 'make yourself at home' can never give the same experience of belonging and richness of association as the experience of the home in which you grew up. The feeling of being at home by is not created by words, but by being there.

All the authors in this book are engaged in analysing people that experience, how unforeseen connections are revealed, how events becomes meaningful and what it feels like to be implicated. We therefore have a collection of essays by readers, narrators, tourists and travellers – people that don't *have* identities, but who create and constantly recreate them. In these studies the concept *culture* is not a package, system or accumulation of texts. There is nothing finished about it. Instead of being the final point, the concept is the starting point for a voyage of discovery. Culture is understood in connection with *cultivation* – with everyday usage, something that groups and individuals actively apply and appropriate to orientate themselves to; feel themselves involved in; to experience the environment around them and make it happen.

The authors of *Being There* refer to a well-known cultural and behavioural scientific tradition. Culture is to be understood *in situ*, starting with the individuals using it. Sometimes events are coherent, clear, present and meaningful – sometimes they roll past blindly like news script on the TV screen. Even the most satisfactory texts remain meaningless if there is no an active reader. How can you find out about the reader's participation? How do you find the active subject in the discussion?

Including Yourself

As implicated, the texts have their invisible counter-texts – or more correctly scientific positions that they want to take one step further. Within ethnology, in Cultural Studies as in other cultural disciplines, the semiotic and linguistic phase, with its roots in the 1980's, led to a fascination with texts, discourses and representations. Within post-structuralism there was a deep presence of the 1970's language-oriented structuralism. The contribution of disciplines like the history of ideas, literature and linguistics became even more inspiring than from the empirical behavioural sciences, from sociology and psychology but also from descriptive ethnography. In addition, the inspiration germinated from this form of linguistic and textually oriented studies also became visible within the disciplines mentioned.

There was an interesting development in ethnology that is worth briefly dwelling on. In books, theses and essays from the 1980's and 1990's, researchers diligently used terms that, in different ways, indicated how language was capable of designating and constructing identities. 'The Cultural Turn', as Victoria Bonnell and Lynn Hunt called the direction in a critical dispute, implied that such dimensions of culture as *things* – *action* and *meaning* disappeared from sight in a jungle of signs, symbols and interpretations. 'If culture or language entirely permeated the expression of meaning, then how could any individual or social agency be identified? Were prisons or clinics, two of Foucault's particular sites of analysis, produced by universally shared mindsets rather than by concrete actions taken in the interest of certain social and political groups? To make a long and complicated story overtly schematic, the cultural turn threatened to efface all reference to social contexts or causes and offered no particular standard of judgement to replace the seemingly more rigorous and systematic approaches that had predominated during the 1960's and 1970's. Detached from their previous assumptions, cultural methods no longer seemed to have any foundation' (Bonnell & Hunt 1999:9).

The authors wanted to get in touch with the social, intersubjective reality. It certainly became problematic when concepts designed to be used in connection with language were applied to action and social relations. The ethnologist Connie Reksten-Kapstad,asks what mistakes were made when culture was viewed as a text that should be read? She answers: 'Culture became regarded as an expression – that is to say the finished result' (Reksten-Kapstad 2002:11). Agency, however, is always something continuous, in the process. Agency is happening.

As a result of this development it became difficult to comment on how people experienced the world. The individual rather became a 'subject position', and the experience became an 'interpellation' where 'the discourse' implicated how it was structured and how bodies were made up in different fields of power. The researchers made a virtue out of establishing that the eventual reality that was behind the discourse was not something they could comment on.

That particular line had to be understood in its context. The wealth of analyses of 'hyphenated cultures' – declarations of how people 'lived their cultures' – is still in general use in today's language. The deconstructions of the 1990's and 'Cultural Turn' created a sort of breathing space in relation to undisputed assertions of the easily objectified cultural concept that characterised earlier ethnology. The new analyses opened ethnology to studies of power and influence. It was often combined with a strong political desire to break with existing power structures. The discourse analyses were a refreshing interruption and signified a reorientation, but at the same time researchers readily overlooked how actors make use of already given definitions to 'give as good as you get' and come up with alternative interpretations. The sociologist Alberto Melucci wanted to go a step further than the analyses of power that have their roots in Foucault, Deluze and Gauttari, because they focussed too one-sidedly on the development and administration of subjects. In the reality of complex society there are powerful interests that both 'try to define the meaning of reality *and* the actors or network of actors that use the resources of the same organisations for defining reality in a new way' (Melucci 1992:211).

When you interpret metaphors and symbols as linguistic expressions and representations, there is a risk that the experience is reduced to a reproduction of something predetermined. The text-oriented hermeneutics claiming that the interpretation is in the message is, to a certain extent, true. Weekly magazines, TV programmes, advertisements and music can be read as single discourses and as parts of more extensive ones. But at the same time there is a big difference in what the symbols stand for and what happens when they are being used, interpreted or ignored. It is that which makes symbols so tremendously useful in the communication of today's differentiated world. They allow variations in an alleged simplicity.

'Symbols… also allow those who employ them to supply part of their meaning,' writes the anthropologist Anthony Cohen, who developed his approach within the line that later came to be known as 'cognitive anthropology.' (It builds on a foundation similar to phenomenology and is actually very distant from the language-based ethno-methodology that developed in the USA in the 1960's). And Cohen continues: 'Symbols do not so much express meaning as give us the capacity to make meaning' (1994:15). Just because people share symbols they do not give them the same meaning. It is just through their vagueness that symbols become so effective, explains Cohen. 'They are, therefore, ideal media through which people can speak a 'common language', behave in apparently the same ways, participate in the 'same' rituals, pray to the 'same' gods, wear similar clothes, and so forth, without subordinating themselves to a tyranny of orthodoxy.' (1994:21).

Certainly people are both creators and reproducers at the same time. But every time an object, a text or a symbol is acquired or learned their content and meaning might be changed. Cohen points out that there is something composite and innovative in this acquisition. There is the shoulder-shrugging 'Oh I see' – as well as the flashing 'Aha!' Connections that were not previously apparent are revealed and insights are awakened. Seen through such a filter, this implies that culture is characterised by mobility, adaptability and a constraint to the situations where it arises. Culture is not a container, but moves, as the anthropologist Kathleen Stewart pointed out, in constant 'fits and starts'. It must be connected to the study of 'practices subject to social use and thus filled with moments of tension, digression, displacement, excess, deferral, arrest, contradiction, immanence and desire'. Any meaning of signs and forms becomes discoverable only in their social and historical usage (Stewart 1996:139).

Reality, as the Norwegian anthropologist Odd Aare Berkaak emphasises, is constantly 'about to happen' (1993). In general people are in that self-explanatory but indefinable feeling of being on the verge of something just about to happen. You therefore need to keep all your senses open and your wits about you. That does not mean that what is to come is clearly loaded with expectations or disappointments – but that you anticipate what may happen more than you actually know it. It is also this interpretation that Gaston Bachelard puts into the word *poetics*, which in turn goes back to the concept of *poiesis*. Of course this is not something that merely characterises contemporary worlds, but it is in everything that is culturally creative. The life-world is both demarcating and open.

The study of practice can only partly start with what it is intended to become, rather than what it became. Culture, as it is understood in this book is also about how meaning and connection are created and conveyed. And meaning is created, as the ancient Greeks said, both through *praxis* and *poiesis*. For Aristotle, praxis was always related to discernment and practical wisdom – *phronesis* – while poiesis was tied to art and creativity – *techne*. You can only have *phronesis* through experience, through action and co-operation. It is therefore a question of experience – preferably in existential terms – of what every one of us should do in order to be socially competent. Nobody else can love for you; you must do that yourself – in the first person singular. It is not anything that can be taught as a subject in the school curriculum. We do not necessarily need to articulate social competence. It is, in general terms, what Michael Polanyi talked about as 'tacit knowledge' (Polanyi 1966) and Peter Smith as 'personal knowledge' (Smith 1973). Practical knowledge is a kind of elementary 'know how' in that intersubjective life that can only be conveyed by the actors themselves who take part and experience what the thing is actually about – *die Sache selbst* – things as they are (Jackson 1996). That is the point that both Francine Lorimer and Kirsti Mathiesen Hjemdahl make in their studies when they take up the subject of children's knowledge and actions.

For Aristotle, the *poietical* disciplines were also action oriented. Their aim was to portray something, to create. That can be done through artistic representation and therefore poetry comes in here. But it also actually happens when people manufacture objects – material culture – *techne*. The new phenomenology consequently strives to study how people in their actions open the world both through praxis and *poiesis*.

Actually it is possible that the *poietical* dimension, as presented by philosophers like Heidegger and Bachelard, gives us a deeper understanding of language than that which is expressed through 'the linguistic turn'. Language is an opening that lets things as they are come to words. In language we also convey what we are 'attuned' to and how we are 'attuned'. Reality does not reach us as in an objective way, but is all the time filtered through our moods. Moods are disclosers: 'they show us things in a more fundamental way than theoretical positions ever can'. We are always attuned in some way to our overall situation (Polt 1999:66). And through this we either expose or cover up what we are. In his investigation of Istria, Jonas Frykman points out how poetical language can, in this way, contribute to a new understanding of the political realities.

Defending Vagueness

When the everyday is focussed upon it means that the investigations become somewhat more complex. Not that they are more difficult or advanced, but rather less clear-cut, less customised and harder to generalise from. Perhaps the study of culture actually has more to do with art than with science, as the sociologist, Sten Andersson, provocatively says in his book *Känslornas filosofi* (The Philosophy of Feelings) (1992). There are no templates, ready answers or clear-cut connections that you can usually associate with 'proper' science, which looks for rules and predictability. Any scholar engaged in studies of culture ought to be liberated from such a scientific ideal. What distinguishes a closely human, hermeneutic science is that it is occupied with questions that in principle are unsolvable. They cannot 'be captured in some universal formula, just like you cannot decide once and for all how you should paint a portrait or a landscape or how people in a novel should act or what a perfect poem should look like' (Andersson 1992:107). By their very nature, the problems that ethnologists work with are *divergent* – they point in many different directions. Many other sciences work with *convergent* problems – finding answers to questions that can be solved with sufficient application of resources, time and intelligence. Surprisingly enough, the intention to look at how discourses have produced identity or culture resembles a desire to make ethnology into a science that works with convergent problems. What really separates ethnology from art is that science has to work with well-defined concepts and theories. In that way, the connection to the phenomenological tradition is something that gives coherence and makes it possible to question well-established methods of analysis and understanding.

In order to paint a fair portrait of the agent, the one who experiences, the researcher is also helped by bringing the environment in which the identity takes shape to the fore – returning to the relationships, social and material where the studied phenomenon takes place. Culture always appears in a state of vagueness – against an environment of fellow beings, shared feelings and fellow actions. If it is not held up against this rich context, culture risks losing its sensuality as well as its bodily-ness – its materiality and spatiality, and actually its life-bearing vagueness. This is how 'culture' becomes abstract. The actors of flesh and blood disappear because the world that they are surrounded by falls outside the frame. As the philosopher Jan Bengtsson points out, everything that people meet is an 'environment-thing' – related to a certain setting, and the environment itself is always tied to the people and their intentions (Bengtsson 1998:233).

Despite appearing as if the discourse analyses and semiotically inspired analyses of culture stand out as contrasts, it is not the intention of the authors of this book to substitute one for the other. That makes a false opposition. Instead the intention is to work cumulatively, to make the picture more effective by actualising the experienced context around the subject. Hermeneutics in its broader sense only deals with text interpretation to a limited extent. It rather focuses on empathy, familiarity, commitment and understanding – the art of reaching an understanding, says Andersson. It 'follows from the fact that you have to work with divergent problems, that is relationships that different people in different situations interpret in different ways (Andersson 1992:110).

What the authors exemplify in their contributions are various ways of pointing to the 'thingness' of things, the 'placeness' of places and the 'human-ness' of individuals. When the word *culture* is used in the active sense, it means that the researcher takes an interest in how people are implicated sensually and bodily as well as rationally. It implies that the vague, the inexact and that which is not clearly formulated should be taken into account. The impulses, the pictures and the imagination often precede thoughts. The language that captures that experience is always more impoverished than the experience itself in all its vagueness.

In the Life-World

There are many different directions to take in order to understand how culture finds meaning for the individual. One way is to start from his or her *life-world* – the human and material environment where meaning is created in a continuous activity. The things included are as obvious as the theme park's houses; the place as close as the beach in Dubrovnik. Phenomenological analyses are generally directed towards studying the experience in its 'immediacy, before it is subject to theoretical elaboration or conceptual systematising', writes Michael Jackson (1996:2). The immediacy of the life-world makes it invisible – concealed because it has a veil of obviousness over it. We do not see what we have under our noses.

Hage refers to Pierre Bourdieu, Michael Jackson brings Hanna Arendt to life, Kjell Hansen actualises Alfred Schutz and Maurice Merleau-Ponty, Jonas Frykman refers to Martin Heidegger and Gaston Bachelard and so on. These are philosophers who, as a matter of course, have all started from the concept or phenomenon of the life-world. It is – with a tautology – the ordinary and quite ambiguous everyday life that people live in. Here life is immediate and 'spontaneous' – and thus relatively unplanned – while interpretations and reflections appear afterwards. It is a practical world, something that the individual acts in – not to the same degree a theoretically reflecting world. It is about the immediate relationships to the environment.

In posing questions about the life-world, the researcher does not need to be engaged in relations *between* the subject and the world but can concentrate on how the subject is created just in the intercourse with the world. There is a highly fictitious boundary between subject and the world around – a kind of unprepared state that is dependent on the person being in the middle of a meaningful whole where people and objects are understood by the intentions of the person involved. *Living* in this world is therefore a deeper existential experience than *knowing*, says Martin Heidegger. Experiences, adventures and possibilities announce themselves more unexpectedly than a ready made interpretation that the subject carries with him or her. It is open, means Heidegger, since thoughts and interpretations are simply there as working *tools* or equipment – not as ends in themselves.

The life-world needs to be adaptable to so many different situations – to working life, the family, shopping at the supermarket and Sunday's sport. In that world we are receptive and curious, constantly ready to turn aside and above all to take action. The ambiguity is its very breath of life. Thing and person mutually constitute each other in this world. *Who* you are is very much about *where* you are and the materiality that you surround yourself with.

According to Edmund Husserl, the life-world is pre-reflexive. It is 'the forgotten foundation that always already precedes and is presupposed by all the scientific research and philosophical thoughts' (Bengtsson 1998:232). Alfred Schutz names it the *pre-phenomenal* and 'only the reflected life is phenomenal' (Bengtsson 1998:64). Both Husserl and Schutz call that normal worldly consciousness the 'natural attitude'. 'In the natural attitude, objects and experiences are encountered as a flux of indistinct and vague shadows. It is only when we move into the reflective attitude that things get endowed with meaning' (Lash 1999:140).

For Bachelard, this is a world where a wealth of images, fancies and dreams precede thought, language and logic. Thus this *experienced* space is never indifferent, never predictable. Predictability is reached when first intersected by the rules of geometry and measures, says Bachelard (2000:20,37).

You cannot easily transcend the life-world – since it is the reality in which you move about. Thus it is something you think *with* rather than think *about*. It is not the frame around our life, rather it is the strokes of the brush that make the things in the painting hang together. Within it we act, think, believe and create. It is, as the philosopher Richard Polt writes, 'a system of purposes and meanings that organizes our activities and our identity, and within which entities can make sense to us' (1999:54). We are not and never can be radically detached from that world. However, with all its limitations the life-world is open – its very vagueness lets things happen and gives meaning to our actions without us needing to interpret it.

In many ways, the concept of life-world reminds us about how once upon a time in ethnology and anthropology the word *culture* was used – the reality that is obvious and unproblematic. As water is to fish, it is just as vital and just as invisible (Frykman & Löfgren 1979). The difference is that the life-world is moving all the time in contraction and expansion. Furthermore it has a pre-cultural presence based more on practical actions than what is included in the concept of culture.

Pierre Bourdieus' quite hackneyed concept of *habitus* implies bodily habits, taste and valuations. It still works as a good peda-gogic example of how to grasp at the wider context around the individual – the life-world that is at the same time closed and open – within which experiences are made. Habitus comes from *habere,* which in Latin means posture, outer condition, figure, nature and overall impression. At the end of the 19th Century it was mainly used in medical contexts to talk about people's type of constitution – asthenic, pyknic, athletic etc. It referred to an embodied quality, something that is already present together with something that is acquired. Habitus is created from the past, moves in the present and stretches towards the future.

In later behavioural scientific application the concept also com-prised social and material experiences. But it still denoted a relatively invisible and vague part of people's ways of orienting themselves in the world. To use Bourdieu's expression, habitus can be seen as a 'structuring structure'. Certain things become meaningful for people with certain experiences. Through the concept of habitus it becomes clearer that people are intellectually but also bodily and sensually formed by the circumstances in which they live. They always strive to build a meaningful whole from the impulses they are exposed to – they see the world through the grid that their habitus provides.

Bourdieu stands in the philosophical and phenomenological tra-dition in which the term *life-world* is used to represent a vaguely designed pre-theoretical world of experiences and adventures. He is strongly inspired by Maurice Merleau-Ponty, Jean Paul Sartre and

Martin Heidegger (Broady 1990).[3] Bourdieu puts an emphasis on social and economic conditions when defining habitus. It appears almost as a Marxist 'superstructure' on a socio-economic base. To a certain extent that approach can be understood with regard to the time that the theories were launched. In other words it is the 1960's and 70's obsession with studying how social and economical structures were expressed and made permanent through culture.

The very vagueness in people's lived world creates a readiness for action. They think with it but hardly about it, in the same way as they think with symbols rather than think about them. The life-world could be compared with how Jean Paul Sartre talked about *being*. It is a totality, or *être en-soi* – a fairly undifferentiated self-identity – 'being is undifferentiated, pure self-identity' (Moran 2000:385). Being is opaque to itself, brute, inert, neither active nor passive… pure immanence, he says in *Being and Nothingness*.

For Maurice in Ghassan Hage's essay, Lebanon is a part of his life-world. When he reads about the Prime Minister he thinks with that. It is the total person that reads. And when he reads, the concrete world of home stands out for him, not as a fixed entity but as an open, vague world that is constantly ajar – ready to take in new ideas and events. Clear opinions, statements and the establishing of ready-formed thought patterns or identities are actualised when they are provoked. Such worlds can be of a longer or shorter duration. When Maja Povrzanovic Frykman describes the *ad hoc* community created during the coach journey, she portrays that web of outer limitations and possibilities, transforming them to a travelling part of the homeland.

When it is people's life-world that filters reality, the ethnologist also needs to make use of double hermeneutics in order to understand it. He or she must first interpret the meaning that is created by the actors by following the gaze of the beholder. Accordingly the researcher can try to put this in relation to the environment in which those concerned live. Through interviews and fieldwork, a possibility is presented to see how far the actor's eye extends (Gilje & Grimen 1992:180).

In this there is always a moment of inventiveness, intuition, creativity and guessing. It is that which Sten Andersson refers to when he talks about research that deals with divergent problems that are more akin to art than 'pure science'. The text that Maurice has in front of him is about him and also about Lebanon, which makes it into something more comprehensive than the mere text. It is the same Maurice that moves around between work and leisure, between love and hate, Sydney and Beirut. What a rich world of life experiences is actualised in the moment of reading the Lebanese newspaper!

But Maurice's life can also be seen in terms of texts or discourses to be read in the newspaper columns. It is the analyses that are often pursued from the textual starting point. Yet the fact that the texts are initial openings to a familiarity of his relationship to the country does not mean that in themselves they are sufficiently substantial. The complexity of the whole is a puzzle where the individual becomes a result of the pieces that are there to interpret. In other words, the actor's subjectivity needs to be taken into consideration.

Making Use of Culture

The practical starting point that unites the multiplicity is the authors' interest in studying culture in use – culture as a series of constantly progressive sequences of action and practice – the *now* of culture. Culture is not there as some demarcated whole but is something that people continually create and understand through their lives (Gerholm & Gerholm 1989). Seen in grammatical terms the analyses make a mental note that culture can be seen as a verb in the *present participle* as something continuous – having a direction, an intention. It is not a substantive in either the definite or the indefinite form, singular or plural: *the* culture, *the* discourse, *and the* symbol. Culture is something more active than a text in the newspaper – it is the newspaper read*ing*. It is not the narrative but rather the hazardous that glimmers in the actual narrat*ing*; not the Croatian identity that is en route through Europe but an ethnic kinship that develops during the travell*ing*. It is not what the things *are* but how they are practically used, forming meaning and coherence for someone in a certain context. In turn, the fact that they exist also actively influences those that use them. Love can be interesting enough to study as a phenomenon, but what are the worlds that are opened for the lover? The car is a fascinating study object, but what surface actions stand out for the driver? For those who are engaged in form and aesthetics, hand-woven textiles can be a distinct object of study. But what is it that the weaver actually works into the fabric? By understanding culture as a verb in the present participle, the researcher concentrates on the consequences of actions; their effects more than their causes. This in no way excludes the importance of studying culture as a noun, but that approach adds to the dimension of how it is made use of.

In order to return to the 'linguistic turn', but from another angle, seeing culture from the aspect of use can be compared with Merleau-Ponty's argument about how we use language. Of course language consists of lots of nouns – of signs and sentences, of discourses, stories, texts and more or less private vocabulary, he says. But whether we write or speak, the vital question is about how we use words – not our actual stock of words or clauses. Language is not an articulation of a prepared thought, or arising from some model. It is the 'accomplishment of the thought itself. The orator does not think before speaking, nor even while speaking; his speech is his thoughts', he says: 'Our possession of language is a matter of how we use words, not our possession of a stock of words '(Merleau-Ponty 2002, Moran 2000:425). To speak is a real speaking act, it involves the senses and the whole body – a *skill* that you rely on and that you can practice. Thus consciousness, says Merleau-Ponty, is not in the first place a matter of that 'I *think*', but than 'I *can*' (Moran 2000:431).

To some degree this approach ties in with the sociologist Ervin Goffman's term *performance,* with the distinction that Goffman wants to make this into a relation where certain individuals appear in front of others who become onlookers to react to, judge and reward. One could say that the actor allows him or herself 'to happen' – or to stage 'a happening'. Less specifically but more fundamentally it is present as an accomplished approach when the philosopher Gaston Bachelard uses the word *poetic* synonymously with how people make the world happen, create meaning and content in the encounter of the subject with the world around. Bachelard was engaged above all with picture, poetry and the creative imagination, but for him reading was synonymous with how consciousness and any knowledge production functioned. 'Bachelard presents a poem not as a cultural or linguistic phenomenon but as a personal experience. A poem is not something that confirms a pre-existing body of knowledge, a theory or a hypothesis; it is an "explosive", a shattering and shaking of our foundations' (McAllester Jones 1991:12).

Like language, culture is always situated somewhere; it forms part of a wider context and brings it to the fore. People that use language, objects or relations are part of some context. And as the context constantly develops, the particular must be adapted to a number of new contexts. But it would be as much a mistake to deduce the culture from the context, as to believe that you can ask the individual for an answer.

Neither culture nor identity exists in either of the poles. Perhaps Merleau-Ponty emphasises more consistently than anyone else that the researcher's attention should neither be put on the individual nor on the surrounding, but just on the *intertwining* – the interwoven tapestry between the body and the world. In this more or less diffuse space new combinations constantly appear. Something new is created all the time with the point of departure in the very bodily intercourse with the world around. This focus on the intertwining space also explains why the study of place has had such a predominant role in ethnological work during the last few years,; 'Given that culture manifestly exists, it must exist somewhere, and it exists more concretely and completely in places than in minds or signs,' writes Edward Casey (1996:33).

The virtual actions are in themselves knowledge generating. 'The activity of using and making is a better clue than the activity of studying and knowing, which is a more specialized and less "everyday" activity. The everyday environment provides an excellent opportunity to recognize ourselves as engaged actors who dwell in the world as a significant whole', says Richard Polt in an interpretation of Martin Heidegger's *Sein und Zeit* (Polt 1999:50).

Dwelling

In *Being and Time* Heidegger made a full-frontal attack on subjectivism and objectivism. He maintained that a human being is not related to the world as a Cartesian subject to an object. The philosophical question is, therefore, not how the subject comes to know the object, which would be the traditional question in Western epistemology. Before any epistemological questions can be addressed, it needs to be recognised that a human being is always 'being-there' (*Da-sein*). In other words, human being is being-in-the-world. Man is always already contextually situated in sociality and materiality. 'The world is not just a place where Dasein happens to be – it is an inseparable part of Dasein's Being' (Polt 1999:64). Heidegger later concluded that *Being and Time* reflected some subjectivist prejudices and perceived the book as some kind of dead end. However, in his later works Heidegger always tried, in different ways, to clarify what he meant by being-in-the-world, often using poetry as an explanatory approach to Being as such. He also began to develop his own poetical thinking in order to come to grips with our situatedness in the world, as for example in the famous lecture 'Building, dwelling, thinking' (*Bauen, Wohnen, Denken*) in 1951. Of course it is not possible to go into Heidegger's later philosophy here, but a short comment may help to clarify what is meant by 'dwelling' and how this notion is related to other Heideggerian ideas.[4]

'To be a human being', Heidegger points out, 'means ... to dwell' (1971:147). Dwelling is how *Dasein* is being-in-the-world. There must, then, be something very special about dwelling. According to Heidegger, dwelling refers us to a *Heimat*, i.e. the place where we are at home, our dwelling-place. We relate to our home in a caring way. Caring-for something happens when we leave that something as it is, or else set it free. The dweller is one who 'lets beings be' (Heidegger 1998:144). This non-instrumental attitude is what Heidegger also refers to as *Gelassenheit*. To accept things as they are – let beings be – does not imply resignation or apathy for him, but rather implies that we take the demands of our earth seriously. And this brings us back to dwelling: *Gelassenheit* and dwelling are, in fact, closely interrelated: 'The fundamental character of dwelling is sparing and preserving' (Heidegger 1998:149). Dwelling, then, can be understood as a kind of 'guardianship', or protection of the earth. It is easy to understand that this philosophy of dwelling can be seen as making way for a new 'poetic' description of the world, and the grounding of a new ecological thinking. This becomes especially clear if we take a closer look at Heidegger's notion of world, or rather 'earth' (*Erde*).

According to Heidegger the world has been locked up in the cage of Western metaphysics. Dwelling is, therefore, an anti-metaphysical move to free the world from such imprisonment and set it free. This 'deep ecology' does not have the atomised individual or Man at the conceptual centre, but rather the earth, the sky, the mortals and the gods. When we are dwelling in this original and existential sense, we do not confront the world in the manner of the metaphysical and scientific tradition of the West. In this tradition, the dominant way of relating surely does not dwell in Heidegger's interpretation of the human condition. In modern society the earth is usually reduced to a resource, and is made available for technological exploitation by scientific means – as a standing reserve. In modernity the enchanted world of things and objects are often disenchanted, and the human being becomes an exploiter of resources. As we are no longer guardians of the world, we are increasingly becoming homeless. Heidegger's new turn towards dwelling is, therefore, a postmetaphysical and postmodernist turn. Postmodernity happens in existential dwelling.

In order to develop a non-metaphysical (and non-scientific) notion of the world that also transcends modernity, Heidegger made use of a new poetical phenomenology where the world is presented as the 'fourfold' (*das Geviert*). 'To dwell', says Heidegger, 'is to belong … within the fourfold of sky and earth, mortals and divinities' (Heidegger 1977: 49, 1971:150). Dwelling, then, is to inhabit the 'fourfold'. A human being exists on the earth, under the sky, among his fellow mortals, and before the gods. Here, we have to limit ourselves to Heidegger's presentation of the earth: '[The] earth is the serving bearer blossoming and fruiting, spreading out in rock and water, rising up in plant and animal' (1971:150).

Obviously, this is not an ethnological, sociological, or physical interpretation of the earth. It is, basically, a poetical description. For Heidegger there is also a close connexion between dwelling and poetical thinking. In Hölderlin's words, often quoted by Heidegger, 'poetically man dwells…' (1971:215). But what does that mean? Poetical thinkers are disclosing the world in new ways for us: They light up the world. Such descriptions can help us to understand what dwelling is. Poets are therefore very important to Heidegger (cf Roth 1996:248–263) as it is the poets, rather than the philosophers, who are developing a new understanding of dwelling on the earth.

To dwell poetically, then, is for us to be open to the sky, the earth, the mortals and the gods, and relate to the 'fourfold' as a guardian – or the 'shepherds of Being'. In other words, dwelling is the *poiesis* and *praxis* of guardianship. It is not easy to translate these insights into ethnology and sociology, but nonetheless, we think, that some recent ethnological contributions hint at what dwelling could be. The Norwegian ethnologist Heidi Richardson (2001) has used the concept of dwelling to show what it is like for actors to dwell on the brink of late modern society. Richardson's 'alternative peasants' are complying with the demands of the earth and refusing to take part in what Heidegger called the 'mechanized food industry' (1977: 15). The alternative farmer does not have to exploit and violate the earth in order to bring forth the potentialities of the soil. In this sense, he is dwelling.

Using Tools

In their essays, the authors operate in contemporary realities – in theme parks, war zones and tourist landscapes. This also indicates that they are engaged in how inspiration from phenomenology becomes a usable tool when they analyse the complex present. Perhaps the usage aspect of culture is in greater demand in a highly technological world. At least it becomes important to pay attention to the role of the thing. We are surrounded by pieces of electronic equipment that 'tend to take on capacities previously associated with subjects: they take on powers of judgement, of measuring, translating and interpretation…' things 'talk, judge, police and seduce' says Scott Lash (1999:342). Then the thing becomes more of a symbol or representation that stands for something else. It is something to think with: something to open up with.

The use of mobile telephones, computers, media covering the whole world and medical technology has certainly created global *cultural codes*, programmes and models and has also given rise to similar experiences, culture bridging *practices* and some silent knowledge. This has developed worlds founded on bodily competence – understanding's everyday operations that embrace earlier differentiating cultures and geographical distance. The mobile telephone in Dubrovnik was keyed in by exactly the same method as in Lund and gave rise to similar social networks. Learning in front of the computer screen means that people can move between countries and continents without crucial technical or operative difficulties. As in the space between people or thing, something happens that cannot be explained from the starting point either of the thing itself or a study of the individual consciousness.

Things are more than an extension of the spheres that people work in. Sartre has written that the body always extends into the tools it uses. 'It is at the end of the stick against which I support myself on the ground, the telescope that reveals the stars for me; it is the chair where I sit and in the entire house I live in, because it is my adaptation of these tools' (Moran 200:385). But they also have repercussions on the user. Gaston Bachelard (1992) thinks that they have a remarkable capacity to be *cultural accelerators*. Something happens in the intervening space. They increase the speed of a course of events just by appearing in a new context. The thing gives rise to both expected and unexpected uses. It holds knowledge and experiences – rituals and traditions develop around it. It also awakens a *response*, a memory in those that use it, something that takes root in the body and mind. Through usage, relation to the thing becomes something personal. 'My' car is, for example, not interchangeable with other cars of the same type and age. Something of it also resounds in me. Is it the smell of the PVC coated fabric or petrol in the cab, the sound of the doors when they slam shut, the purr of the engine, the feeling of sitting in the seats? We all have the experience of stepping into a complete world where you get in 'your' car.

The transportation is not only a journey in space but also in time and environment. From the start, the coach in which immigrants travelled to their homeland became an actor, with its smells, uncomfortable seats and overcrowding, giving the travellers an identity that was difficult to step out of.

But the coach also *provoked*. It was a torment they had to endure. Being together became the starting point for conversation, but also something they ought to disregard. It challenged the travellers' patience and cunning, brought earlier trips and injustices to life. By constantly responding to the thing's provocations, adapting the thing, you integrate it with yourself, writes Bachelard. And when you think, feel and dream you do it with what you work on. Overcoming the thing's resistance makes us conscious of our strength. It wakens the exciting realisation that we can become *something more.* That something more is created by man's active provocation of the world. Human beings can be defined very simply as workers who provoke the world by the instruments of reason and imagination, but also by practically engaging in physical work. The operation of the hand integrates the resisting object with the mind and body of the actual worker and makes him or her realise that the true content of existence is not to *be* but to *become* (Bachelard 1992:39).

Things are certainly active co-creators of culture and sensual chains of meaning and memory are released when things are being used. The worlds they actualise are comprehensive and multidimensional in their very vagueness – open, filled with knowledge, alternatives and possibilities.

It then becomes obvious that things should be noticed as well '*an sich*' as in context – not in a essentialist sense, but as the starting point for action and thinking. For little Aksel, the wonderland came alive when he ran up and down the steps of the Moomin house – willing to open himself to the fascination in the surrounding objects. Mathiesen Hjemdahl describes how the adults that accompanied him slowly discovered that they had been socialised not to allow themselves be captivated. Things deserve to be seen for what they can do; the life and the intelligence that they contain and the challenges they put to their users. And it should of necessity imply that you look at what happens when they are being used.

What the researchers in this book try to exemplify through their studies, is that things – and also in a figuratively transferred sense, culture in general – can be seen as *tools*. Culture certainly exists without its users in the same way as tools do. But what is interesting about tools is that they bring the world to life when applied for distinctive purposes. They create a logic when used and when used they also create the user. It is most logical to claim that the boy entered a separate play-world when he ran among the fairytale figures – 'an otherness' or *alterity.* The outcome of such a perspective would be to maintain that this was a ritually demarcated space with its special rules for the game and experience – he became the game, so to speak, where the actual subject was not the individual but the game in itself (Reksten-Kapstad 2001:16, Bernstein 1991:173). But you can also maintain that he opened himself to the multiplicity of the object's message. Images of witches that fly up like sparks in the air allow the child to see and wonder; to put two and two together. Certain facets of the world are revealed to them.

When culture is seen as a tool it becomes synonymous with the knowledge and skills that people use in everyday activities, to orientate, create context and meaning. Culture sometimes opens to the new and different and sometimes to the well known and predictable. There is a lot of continuity in gloom and routine.

To see culture as a tool thus makes it into something you use to discover and understand. It is generally used to figuratively 'catch' and to act. For example, that which draws hundreds of thousands of people every summer to a region like Istria is not merely what the region in itself *is*, but what *happens* to those that go there. If it had not been used in a creative way in everybody's attempt to explore a self-identity, or being part of their search for what they as yet do not have, visiting the place would hardly be rewarding. The discourse that is now taking form about the region's special character puts the emphasis on the open, the unformulated, that which awaits.

The studies that were put before the seminar at the Inter University Centre in Dubrovnik during this well tuned week in October came from fieldwork. The researchers had been there in person, had sat in the coach, stood on the steps of the museum, visited the camp for amputees and followed the children home from the midsummer bonfire. Similar fieldwork could very well be carried out in archives, museums or through pictures or written sources. The emphasis is on the method, on the intentions of looking in the same direction as the persons in question and of using oneself in the process of interpretation. It is usually said that in ethnology, regeneration appears every time that people have a longing to go to the field, whether it is in contemporary society or in the past. To expose yourself to the possibilities and the limitations that people live with usually means a deeper understanding and the possibility of breaking out of your own stuffiness. In order to make words and analyses capture what you experience, good tools are needed. Indeed scientific theories are parts of the working equipment that open the world and deserve to be examined for the new knowledge they can present.

Notes

1   This quote is from Alfons Grieder's interview with Hans-Georg Gadamer, 'On Phenomenology' (Palmer 2001:113).

2   Some of the essays in Hansen & Salomonsson 2001 appear in slightly modified form in English in *Ethnologia Europaea* 2002,32:2. The uniting theme for this issue is the different approaches to place, although not all of them are working from a phenomenological point of view.

3   For Bourdieu the concept of habitus could also work as a sociological commentary upon Sartre's existentialist philosophy. In his book on Heidegger (Bourdieu 1991) he remains one of the most ardent critics of Heidegger's ontology (cf Safranski 1998).

4   Julian Young's article 'What is dwelling? The Homelessness of Modernity and the Wordling of the World', in *Heidegger, Authenticity and Modernity: Essays in Honour of Hubert L. Dreyfus,* Cambridge: MIT Press, 2000, vol. 1, pp: 187-203. See also Young's book *Heidegger's Later Philosophy,* Cambridge: Cambridge University Press, 2002.

References

Andersson, Sten 1992: *Känslornas filosofi.* Göteborg: Daidalos.
Bachelard, Gaston. 1964/94: *The Poetics of Space* 1964/94. Boston: Beacon Press.
Bachelard, Gaston 1992:. *Jorden och drömmerier om vila.* Lund: Skarabé.
Bengtsson, Jan 1998: *Fenomenologiska utflykter: människa och vetenskap ur ett livsvärlds-perspektiv.* Göteborg: Daidalos.

Berger, Peter & Luckmann, Thomas 1996: *The Social Construction of Reality*. Middlesex: Penguin Books.

Berkaak,Odd Aare & Even Ruud 1992: *Den påbegynte virkelighet. Studier i samtidskultur* Oslo: Universitetsforlaget.

Berglin, Elisabeth. 2000: *En bonadsmålare och hans värld. Johannes Nilsson i Breared.* Apostrof: Lund.

Bernstein, R.J. 1991: *Bortom objektivism och relativism. Vetenskap, hermeneutik och praxis.* Göteborg: Daidalos.

Bonnell, V.E. & L. Hunt 1999: *Beyond the Cultural Turn: New Directions in the Study of Society and Culture.* Berkeley: University of California Press.

Bourdieu, Pierre 1991: *The Political Ontology of Martin Heidegger.* Stanford: Stanford University Press.

Broady, Donald 1990: *Sociologi och epistemologi. Om Pierre Bourdieus författarskap och den historiska epistemologin.* Stockholm: HLS Förlag.

Burstedt, Anna 2002: The Place on the Plate! *Ethnologia Europaea* 32:2, pp: 145–158.

Casey, Edward. 1996: How to Get from Space to Place in a Fairly Short Stretch of Time: Phenomenological Prolegomena. In: Feld, Steven & Keith H: Basso (eds) *Senses of Place.* Santa Fe: School of American Research Press.

Cohen, Anthony P. 1989: *The Symbolic Construction of Community.* London: Tavistock Publications Ltd.

Frykman, Jonas 2001: Belonging in Europe Modern Identities in Minds and Places. Niedermüller, Peter & Bjarne Stoklund (eds) *Europe. Cultural Construction and Reality.* Museum Tusculanum Press. University of Copenhagen. pp: 13–24.

Frykman, Jonas 2002: Place for Something Else: Analysing a Cultural Imaginary. *Ethnologia Europaea* 32:2, pp: 47–68.

Frykman, Jonas & Orvar Löfgren 1979: *Den kultiverade människan.* Lund: Liber.

Frykman, Jonas & Peter Niedermüller 2002: Getting Europe into Place. *Ethnologia Europaea* 32:2, pp: 3–6.

Gerholm, Lena 1985: *Projektkultur och kulturprojekt: En fallstudie av en kulturpolitisk försöksverksamhet.* Malmö: LiberFörlag.

Gerholm, Lena & Tomas Gerholm 1989: Om inte kultur fanns, så skulle man behöva uppfinna den. *Nord Nytt 37*, s. 8–16.

Gilje, Nils & Harald Grimen 1992: *Samhällsvetenskapernas förutsättningar,* Göteborg: Daidalos.

Hansen, Kjell 2002: Festivals, Spatiality and the new Europe. *Ethnologia Europaea* 32:2, pp: 19–36.

Hansen, Kjell & Karin Salomonsson (eds) 2001: *Fönster mot Europa. Platser och identiteter.* Lund: Studentlitteratur.

Hastrup, Kirsten et al 1975: *Den ny antropologi.* Borgen/Basis.

Heidegger, Martin 1971: *Poetry, Language, Thought,* New York: Harper and Row.

Heidegger, Martin 1977: *The Question Concerning Technology and other Essays,* New York: Harper and Row.

Heidegger, Martin 1998: *Pathmarks,* Cambridge: Cambridge University Press.

Hjemdahl, Kirsti Mathiesen 2003: *Tur/retur temapark – oppdragelse, opplevelse, kommers.* Kristiansand: Høyskoleforlaget.

Jackson, Michael 1996 (ed.): *Things as They Are: New Directions in Phenomenological Anthropology.* Bloomington: Indiana University Press.

Lash, Scott 1999: *Another Modernity: A Different Rationality.* Oxford: Blackwell.

Lindqvist, Mats 1987: *Klasskamrater. Om industriellt arbete och kulturell formation 1880–1920.* Stockholm: Carlssons.

Lindqvist, Beatriz 1991: *Drömmar och vardag i exil. Om chilenska flyktingars kulturella strategier.* Stockholm: Carlssons.

McAllester Jones, Mary 1991: *Gaston Bachelard, Subversive Humanist. Texts and Readings.* Madison: The University of Wisconsin Press.

Melucci, Alberto 1992: *Nomader i nuet. Sociala rörelser och individuella behov i dagens samhälle.* Göteborg. Daidalos.

Melucci, Alberto 1991: *Nomads of the Present: Social Movements and Individual Needs in Contemporary Society.* Philadelphia: Temple.

Nielsen, Niels-Kayser 1997: Movement, Landscape and Sport. Comparative Aspects of Nordic Nationalism Between the Wars. *Ethnologia Scandinavica* 27.

Palmer, Richard E. 2001: *Gadamer in Conversation: Reflections and Commentary. Hans-Georg Gadamer.* New Haven: Yale UP.

Polanyi, Michael 1973: *The Tacit Dimension,* Gloucester, Mass.

Polt, Richard 1999: *Heidegger: An Introduction.* London: UCL Press

Povrzanovic Frykman, Maja 2002: Violence and the Re-Discovery of Place. *Ethnologia Europaea* 32:2, pp: 69–88.

Reksten-Kapstad, Connie 2001: *Når handling tar plass. Ein kulturstudie av fellesaksjonen mot Gasskraftverk.* Bergen: Det historisk-filosofiske fakultet.

Reme, Eva: Exhibition and Experience of Cultural Identity. The Case of Bergen – European City of Culture. *Ethnologia Europaea 32:2,* pp: 37–46.

Richardson, Heidi 2000: *Tillbake ti jorda: drömmer oog hverdagsliv: en etnologisk studie med utganspunkt i 1970-talets alternativbønder.* Bergen: Det historisk-filosofiske fakultet.

Roth, Michael 1996: *The Poetics of Resistance: Heidegger's Line,* Evanston, Ill.: Northwestern University Press.

Safranski, Rüdiger 1998: *Martin Heidegger: Between Good and Evil.* Cambridge, Mass. Harvard University Press.

Shore, Bradd 1996: *Culture in Mind. Cognition, Culture, and the Problem of Meaning.* New York and Oxford: Oxford University Press.

Smith, Peter 1966: *Personal Knowledge.* London: Routledge.

Stewart, Kathleen 1996: An Occupied Place. In: Feld, Steven & Keith Basso (eds): *Senses of Place.* Santa Fe: School of American Research Press.

MAJA POVRZANOVIĆ FRYKMAN

Bodily Experiences and Community-Creating Implications of Transnational Travel

In connection to the processes of national identification in wartime, I argued (Povrzanović 1997) that the embodiment of experience is crucial in the analysis of the cultural outcomes of the lived encounters with violence, when the body 'appears as a threatened vehicle of human being and dignity' (Csordas 1994:4).* In the situations in which violence constitutes a new reality, people focus on the here and now and prioritize the physical aspects of body before the social ones. Such a here-and-now presence secludes the persons exposed to the same deprivations and fears from those from the 'outer world' who do not share their experience. At the same time, it creates a space recognised as being authentic and providing a sense of community (Povrzanović 1997:159).

I believe that something similar, although less extreme, is happening during the long bus rides by which people positioned as *immigrants* connect different places of their belonging – those in the countries of origin and those in which they live in Western Europe. It is in those places, but also in the very practices of connecting them, where their identities are situated. These connecting practices are creating what Thomas Faist (2000:200) defines as transnational social spaces consisting of 'combinations of sustained social and symbolic ties, their contents, positions in networks and organizations, and networks and organizations that can be found in multiple states'.[1]

Alejandro Portes and co-authors (1999) distinguish *economic*, *political* and *socio-cultural transnationalism*, thus offering a useful working typology that helps in organising and interpreting what otherwise would be a chaotic set of activities collected in empirical research. A second distinction they propose is between *transnationalism from above*, i.e. transnational activities initiated and conducted by powerful institutional actors, such as multinational corporations and states, and *transnationalism from below*, which is the result of the less institutionalized initiatives by immigrants and their home country counterparts.

The scholarly interest in the empowering potentials of transnational practices can be understood in the context of 'discovering' the 'high intensity of exchanges, the new modes of transacting and the multiplication of activities' (Portes et al. 1999:219) that migrants sustain across borders. Namely, their exchanges became visible as they gained a systematic quality and an unprecedented range due to the modern technology-based possibilities of communication via telephone and e-mail, transport of people, money, goods, news, and accessibility of all kinds of media products.[2]

Yet, however complexly articulated localities become in transnational economic, political, and cultural flows, states still hold the coercive power within their borders, and the social construction of place is still 'a process of local meaning-making, territorial specificity, juridical control, and economic development' (Guarnizo and Smith 1998:12). The condition of *disadvantage* to the dominant logic of the world economy – the immigrants' (or transmigrants') as well as of the people in their home countries engaged in transnational practices – is *differentia specifica* of their position.

Methodological Concerns

The notions of transmigrants and transnational social fields are of great analytical value. Yet, some aspects of their transnational lives, like border crossings which reduce people to 'wrong' passports, might have 'essentializing' consequences for people's self-understanding.

In an important analysis of epistemological and political implication of the discourse of 'identity' in the US academy, Roger

Rouse (1995) recognises the novelty of anthropological analyses of multi-local identities situated in transnational social spaces. They are understood neither as markers of transition (towards assimilation) nor as signs of pathology (in the limbo of in-betweenness), but 'as lasting and intelligible responses to the varied pressures people face' (Rouse 1995:354). However, he points out that 'in many cases, (im)migrants continue to ground politically important claims in the assertion and revalorization of identities that are both singular and localized' (Rouse 1995:355). From this perspective,

> those who celebrate migrants as exemplars of multiplicity and de-territorialization are guilty of *bad ethnography* because they fail adequately to listen and observe, and *bad politics* because they privilege the allure of current intellectual fashion, especially the metaphors of post-structuralist theory and the imagery of a literary postmodernism, over the practical realities of (im)migrants' lives and struggles (Rouse 1995:355).

If 'one of the most complicated components to investigate is that of the micro-dimension of transnationalism' (Guarnizo and Smith 1998:26) – 'micro' referring to personal experiences – I believe that here lies the possibility of a specific contribution of qualitative methodology bringing about ethnographies of grass-roots aspects of transnationalism and the individual experiences thereof.

The ethnographic insights in this essay should therefore be understood as being an entrance or starting point to several different trails of insights (cf. Marcus 1995): through the travellers' personal histories and the stories that bus drivers might tell about their passengers; through the objects that are brought along, bought during the course of the journey and planned to be brought back – in both directions; through the situations of togetherness and of conflict in the bus; and finally, although the list is far from exhausted, through the narratives of everyday experience or memories that are shared between people during the bus rides. The starting point character of these hints should be stressed here, for any such trail, of course, needs to be elaborated.

The ethnography that follows is not complex enough for grounding a thorough analysis; it should provide insights and raise some methodological questions. My intention is to show not only that bodily practices assessed *in situ* provide ethnographic material that is complementary to the material that can be gained through interviews, but also that a phenomenological approach may be crucial for understanding some identification processes in transnational social spaces. As proposed by Michael Jackson (1983), practical mimesis – in this case, sharing the travel experience – forms the grounds of an emphatic understanding.

> For by using one's body in the same way as others in the same environment, one finds oneself informed by an understanding which may then be interpreted according to one's own custom or bent, yet which remains grounded in a field of practical activity and thereby remains consonant with the experience of those among whom one has lived (Jackson 1983:340–341).

I will describe two bus rides between Sweden and Croatia by the company that regularly (once a week) connects several towns in Sweden with the Croatian capital Zagreb. People using this connection are predominantly Croatian immigrants living in Sweden since the 1960s and Croats who came to Sweden as refugees (mostly from Bosnia-Hercegovina) in the 1990s. As most other buses operating between Sweden and former Yugoslav republics, the one described here is 'ethnic' in the sense that people of the same ethnic affiliation tend to ride the same buses, often driven by and owned by their co-ethnics. The reasons are practical (the final destinations are different), but sometimes also have to do with the ethnic differentiation resulting from the wars in Croatia and Bosnia-Hercegovina in the 1990s.[3]

While presenting my own experience of personal travel as a means of maintaining transnational social fields, I intend to point out the non-chosen or imposed aspects of identity construction, implied in two sets of limits of negotiation and the restrictions of choice.

One is caused by the very means of transportation, which for most travellers is the only financially viable choice, and brings about certain bodily experiences.

The other is defined by the regime of international borders. At the borders, people's multiple identities are 'flattened out' to a single (national) identity materialized in the form of passport. When such crossings are collective (as in the case of a transmigrant bus), there is reason to believe that some kinds of community-creation processes are intensified.

A Personal Memory

On the cold morning of 31 October 1994, the day before All Saints' Day – which in Croatia is devoted to visiting family graves – I was standing at the arrival platform of Zagreb central bus station for more than three hours. I was waiting for a bus from Frankfurt am Main to bring a package sent by my aunt who has lived in Germany since the early 1960s. My memory of that day is extremely vivid, first and foremost for the feeling of nausea and suffocation due to the continuous inhalation of exhaust fumes, but also for the fact that, although freezing, I did not dare to enter the station building: I was afraid of missing 'my' bus. The only way to recognise it among the five buses that arrived from Frankfurt within those three hours was by the number-plate, since the same company ran them all. Not one of them had an exact arrival time. It could not be checked at any of the counters either, but only discussed with more experienced people waiting there with me. Minimum and maximum calculations were made: emptying the bus for a thorough customs check at some of the borders can take hours.

Eventually, a heavy cardboard box containing presents for my children, clothes and household items, was handed over to me. I just had to tell the driver who was sending it, once I had reached him through the excited crowd of people elbowing their way closer to the bus. Those people were leaning over and stepping onto the heaps of suitcases, boxes and bags growing on either side of the bus, trying to get hold of their belongings and organise their own heaps of overloaded luggage. They were hugging their relatives with exclamations of joy, shouting, smiling, sighing and looking tired.

Although I was not then professionally interested in Croatian *Gastarbeiter* (in vernacular Croatian, the German term has been adopted), I remember my own amazement and mixed feelings over the quantity and the variety of objects being taken out of all the buses' orifices. Parts of machines needed in peasant households, a roll of wire fencing, a child-size bicycle, huge boxes of washing powder, plastic bags containing *Made in Germany* toys and oversize packages of sweets were appearing, along with immense quantities of suitcases.

My amazement and mixed feelings were not coming from total lack of experience with *Gastarbeiter* lives. As so many other Croats, I have several extended family members living abroad as economic migrants.[4] It was the number of the buses, arriving one after the other, that 'put things in proportion': it is important to visit the graves on All Saints' Day, and living abroad is not really an excuse for not doing so. They were the items of everyday use: were they carried from Germany to save money, to express care, to show off, to feel needed, to meet obligations, or to try to balance the living standards of post-war Croatia with that of Western Europe? My mixed feelings also included pity: the one long-distance bus trip I had experienced myself made me understand that it can be difficult to endure. My own physical discomfort, due to the long waiting, suddenly seemed complementary to the travellers' obvious exhaustion – we were all engaging in a project of connecting places, which can leave unpleasant bodily memories.

Limits and Constrictions, Abstract and Concrete

In his book *Migrancy, Culture, Identity* (1994), Ian Chambers suggests that the opposition between *here* and *there* may be regarded as a cultural construction:

> An authentically migrant perspective would, perhaps, be based on an intuition that the opposition between here and there is itself a cultural construction, a consequence of thinking in terms of fixed entities and defining them oppositionally. It might begin by regarding movement, not as an awkward interval between fixed points of departure and arrival, but as a mode of being in the world. The question would be, then, not how to arrive, but how

to move, how to identify convergent and divergent movements; and the challenge would be how to notate such events, how to give them a historical and social value (Paul Carter, *Living in a New Country. History, Travelling and Language*, London: Faber & Faber 1992:101, quoted in Chambers 1994:42).

Movement between distant places of attachment certainly is 'a mode of being in the world' for people living in transnational social fields. The 'challenge' of giving the movements 'historical and social value' is already met by the very existence, the ways of functioning and the meanings of those social fields – not only for their active participants, but also for all people affected by them. But the literature celebrating the migrants as examples of multiplicity and de-territorialization (in the vein of the quotation above) may underestimate the limits and constrictions relevant for (or even central to) the migrants' identification processes.[5] Here the strength of ethnographic experience is supreme:

> The breadth of our ethnographic experience offers a scope for imagining political possibilities and social formations that others have not yet considered. But the depth of our ethnographic experience provides a sobering index of a gap between imagining and actualizing these possibilities (Amit-Talai 1998:56).

But, what exactly is implied in the notion of 'ethnographic experience'? In this essay, theoretical claims regarding some aspects of transnational practices are not 'confirmed' by the 'sufficient' amount of material. 'Ethnographic experience' brought forward in this essay implies primarily the researcher's personal – most importantly, bodily – experiences.

Research has shown that there are numerous ways of maintaining a transnational social field, i.e. of connecting places within it (c.f. the relevant references in Povrzanović Frykman 2001a). When it comes to travelling between distant places of attachment, these ways significantly depend on migrants' financial possibilities. It is true that travel has become a mass commodity and is cheaper than it was some decades ago (not to mention the times of European migration to the Americas, when transatlantic travel was a life-project). Yet, among the many people eager to continue being transmigrants, whom I am meeting in Sweden, only bus rides, not air connections, are considered to be cheap, i.e. affordable.

Although, or rather because, travel has become a mass-commodity, it clearly reflects the class relations of today's world – in economic, social and all possible metaphorical senses of class as classification (from business-class waiting lounges to 'non-EU citizens' entrances at airports; from diplomats' limousines to *Gastarbeiter* buses). On the one hand, travel stands for freedom of movement in a literal sense, as well as for metaphorical transgressions, growth and change.[6] On the other hand, hunger and fear have been among the chief motivations for 'travel' in the twentieth century. 'Historically many people have been recruited or coerced to travel neither for leisure, nor interest nor choice' (Curtis and Pajaczkowska 1994:214).

In the literature on transnationalism, travel stands for an active choice of keeping (through face-to-face contacts) transnational so-cial relations. Yet, what happens to, with, and around their bodies is seldom under the control of the travellers themselves. Recent examples of people smuggled into Western European countries and who died before even getting a chance to develop their own versions of transnationalism cannot give a relevant comparison in the framework of this article. Still, such extreme examples of travel with tragic outcomes have a common link with the less dramatic bus rides discussed here, in the restriction of choice and the harsh bodily experience.

By agreeing to become a passenger in a certain type of vehicle and run by a company with a particular profile, one is acquiring not only a matching bodily experience – of seating, temperature, (non)conditioned air, toilets, food, music, treatment by the person-nel, but also a whole package of labels – materialised at the state borders – which make one wonder if any 'taking off' of ascribed identities is easy (or possible at all).

What follows here is a presentation of my impressions and obser-vations made during two trips, from Malmö to Zagreb and back, in November 2000. I was accompanied by my two children and travelling from the place in Sweden where I have lived and worked for the last three years, to my hometown in Croatia, where my family and friends live. Hence, I was not positioning myself as a researcher, but as a (transmigrant) traveller holding a Croatian passport as were most other people on the bus. This article is thus based on fieldwork that consciously relies on observations of non-discursive aspects of the experience of travelling, which are otherwise 'hidden from history'. It is a *post festum* effort to theorise that experience.

Although I was aware of the importance of personal travel in the context of my research in identity formations in diaspora and exile, the salience of the bodily experiences of such travel became obvious to me only after being involved in it. However, I planned and prepared myself for making dual use of the trip, as both a transportation and a fieldwork opportunity. I did not approach people in the bus with questions about their travel experiences, but opened my senses to what was happening around me, and to how I felt myself. I wrote down some observations during the travel; others have been noted later, or simply – remembered. Smells, for example, or the chill, do leave imprints in memory.

The only things that I asked people about were their reasons for travelling to Croatia. Otherwise, I engaged in conversations primarily as a co-passenger, trying to affect the situation as little as possible.[7] Many of the utterances that I overheard were meant to be overheard; people are aware of physical proximities in the bus. Also, for many, talking is the favourite pastime during the travel. It seems to be usual that a more talkative person 'amuses' several people sitting around them. Several stories have been told to 'wider' bus audiences of peoples' experiences of bus rides, smuggling, and encounters with customs controls; approaching a border is the usual context for such kind of narration.

In this essay, a systematic description is not intended, but rather a collection of audio, olfactory and visual experiences constituting a kaleidoscopic image. From another seat in the bus, or on some other date, this image could have been different, but most probably only in the details.

Bodily Experiences and Other Insights

So, what did my bus trips between Malmö to Zagreb look like? Or rather, how did they feel?

Two unpleasant memories are striking: the darkness that prevented me from reading when I was awake and people around me were sleeping, and the smell from the toilet in the lower part of the bus. There was no running water, and the bucket used for flushing it was refilled far too seldom.

I was forced to stay awake, because the chair which was supposed to be folded into an improvised bed above my seat was broken. So, on my way to Zagreb, I spent the night hours half-sitting on a flattened-out double seat with my legs cramped between my two sleeping children, and a man lying next to me on the upper level. Since the 'bed' was as wide as a chair, his body was literally a few centimetres away from my head, touching it whenever the man moved in his sleep. Turned into an image to be shared in this text, the physical touch I experienced can be seen as a key-image of my entire experience of that travel. The unwanted proximity was impossible to escape; it was grounded in both my and my co-passengers' need to travel to the same destination; it created an order specific to that of low-cost transnational bus-travel, which was different from the one in the ordinary world outside the bus.

These were among the last rides the company made with that particular vehicle before purchasing a new one. It was obvious that no repairs and improvements had been made to the bus for a long time. There were no pillows and only three blankets were available (I had taken my own pillows from Sweden and also decided that we should carry our own blankets on the way back from Zagreb). The tiny kitchen in the lower part of the bus was out of service, too. So, no cooked sausages were available, but only coffee and beer, sold for any European currency, but at high prices (that, at least, was how people around me regarded the prices, remembering that coffee was included in the ticket when a Swede owned the company). The hostess just stated the obvious; she did not apologise once. A few people loudly shared their disgust and disappointment, but my general impression was that people accepted anything, knowing that excitement and anger cannot change the circumstances. Many refugees from Bosnia-Hercegovina did not leave Sweden for five years, as that was a precondition for acquiring Swedish citizenship. So, today they are not only the most frequent travellers (every tenth ride is free), but maybe also not very demanding ones. Being able to travel is very important so that people do not consider leaving the bus in protest just because there is no water for the toilet. Although there are at least seven regular lines to Croatia starting from different Swedish towns (plus several 'Bosnian' lines, heading to Bosnia-Hercegovina; some are owned by Swedes and some by Croats and Muslims), there is no real market competition between the companies. All buses seem to be pretty full all the time.

An elderly woman who had come to Sweden as a refugee in the early 1990s fell down the stairs when trying to reach the toilet in the night, when no light was on. In some other circumstances and for some other person, it could have been a reason to sue the company, but it was seen (by her, as well as by the people around her) as bad luck – or even as good luck, for she only hit her face. Returning to Sweden a week later, she had a bruise under her left eye. In the meantime, she attended a wedding in Bosnia, but had to return to Sweden so soon afterwards in order to collect her social care money on a certain date.

A story that I overheard, but could not check, was about a young woman who died shortly after such a bus trip due to blood-circulation problems (better known in relation to intercontinental flights), and the falling of the chair under which I was supposed to sleep made me aware of the physical dangers involved in bus rides. The fact that I, as well as two other people sitting at the front of the bus, hit our heads violently against the TV set while trying to pull things from the luggage which was piled on the floor, confirmed that. A man whom I knew from before told me that he did not travel on the upper deck as he hit his head against the same TV set so hard that he had concussion.

He was on sick leave in Sweden and had to go to Croatia because his aged father needed to be taken care of at home during the first few weeks after an operation. Some other people's reasons for travelling included: visiting relatives who had come to Sweden as refugees;

visiting relatives in Croatia or Bosnia-Hercegovina; spending a month with a daughter (a refugee to Sweden) who had given birth to her first child; attending a relative's wedding in Bosnia, being the representative of the part of the family that had lived in Sweden since the 1990s; returning to Sweden after having done some repairs in the summer house by the Dalmatian coast: the husband coming later by car, while the wife was hurrying to see their newly born Swedish-Croatian grandchild. A young Croatian woman from Bosnia, now living in Sweden, was travelling in order to collect her husband who had finally got a residence permit for Sweden; a Swedish born Croat of similar age was travelling with his father to pick olives in the family olive groves in Dalmatia. A middle-aged Bosnian refugee to Sweden had buried her father in Bosnia and was now returning. A Croat who had been living in Norway for thirty-five years had gone to Croatia to sell some property and to have dental treatment at a much lower price than in Norway. A Croat now retired in Sweden had been to his home-town in Dalmatia to spend a month in his eleven-room summer house and wait for his Swedish-born children and grandchildren to join him at Christmas. Another man had to check the three empty family houses in his home-village in central Croatia: one of his own, and the other two remaining after his and his wife's parents had died. Three young siblings, accompanied by their mother, travelled in order to spend two weeks with their grandparents who had also come to Sweden as refugees, but had returned to Bosnia two years ago. Births, deaths, war events in their home-towns, life in Sweden, good and bad wages in Swedish factories, reminiscences from former bus rides... those are some of the topics that I heard about. Stories about small-scale smuggling seem to be the favourite genre. (They are deliberately shared and not seen as a source of moral concern; cf. also Haller 2000).

'People are suffering', a man said, referring to the very bus ride. There was, however, a humorous tone to it, a kind of a getting-along-with-destiny. When we were half-an-hour away from Zagreb, the atmosphere changed: there was the feeling of celebratory laughter, as if an energy-shot had been pumped into each and every one. When the first Zagreb houses came in sight, people started to pack, put their coats on, stretch their arms and legs – preparing to leave the 'monodimensional' space of the bus and start moving in their own directions, on their own accord.

'Difficult, narrow, wrinkled, stinking – but producing a kind of "we are in this together" feeling', was what I wrote in my notebook during the trip from Malmö to Zagreb. Although the lack of space and the lack of sleep could bring about conflicts, people were patient and helpful. Everyone seemed to be caring for the children, addressing them, offering them food. The only disputes I witnessed were caused by some people who did not want to sleep, i.e. in keeping their beds in the seat position they thus forced the ones behind them to remain sitting upright through the night.

Two men who had met on the bus, gradually became more and more tipsy and sang very loudly for at least two hours. Several people around them were not very pleased, but did not say a word. These two people – coming from Dalmatia and Slavonia respectively (two culturally distinct Croatian regions), and living abroad for more than thirty years – were comparing each other's competence in Croatian folk songs. There was a constant half-tense mocking between these two men who wanted to prove their superiority, through somewhat depreciating undertones based on stereotypes about the two regions they came from. One of them sang a 'Croatian nationalist' song for which he had ended up in jail thirty-five years ago. Politics was suddenly present when he, to a melody of a folk song, improvised a text about Radovan Karadžić, the Bosnian Serbs' leader indeited to the International War Criminal Court in The Hague.

In another way, politics was also present in the moments when we had to show our passports. The sleeping was interrupted, and the hostess suddenly acted as a competent – initiated – messenger of authority: 'Beds up – *they* want you to sit straight!'; 'All of you, have your passports ready!' And there we were, sitting with our passports open, showing the photos to the Austrian police officer, who was looking at us carefully. Walking by in silence, he did not even cast a glance at the few passengers holding Swedish passports; he only uttered: 'OK'. 'Austrian policemen are dangerous', a man said afterwards. (He was experienced, having travelled this route three times a year. After having been scared to death on a bumpy flight from Zagreb to Gothenburg, he decided never to fly again.)

A man in his fifties, holding a Bosnian passport issued in Banja Luka, and having a permanent residence permit in Sweden (and in Australia, where his children had lived since the early 1990s), was not allowed to pass through Austria because he did not have the 'Schengen Visa' in his passport. 'We can't leave the man on the road', the hostess said. It seems to be a border-police established rule that a passenger not allowed to cross the border must be taken back to some petrol-station.

Other passengers were angry with him, or perhaps felt pity for him. The man himself was angry and very stubborn, talking loudly about his two permanent residence permits and claiming that, in his case, asking for the visa was absurd. Instead of paying a certain sum and getting the visa on the spot, he decided to demonstratively leave the bus and proceed from Slovenia by air. Anyway, we all had not only an extra half-an-hour of waiting because of this episode, but also an extra hour of driving back to Slovenia, and then again to Austria. At the border, our passports and our faces were checked once more, in silence, by the police-officer who boarded the bus. Someone commented the next morning: 'Did you see that yesterday? *Hajderovci* (Haider-supporters) – not even "good evening", nothing!'

After yet another border had been passed, the hostess returned our passports, previously collected so that they could be handed to a German police officer: she yelled out our first names only. Every passport was then handed over from person to person, until it reached its owner. No one was anonymous any more, and we all had indisputably Croatian names.

Many passengers addressed the two drivers by their first names, too. During the ride, after the 'ritual' asking for permission, some people who did not know each other, started addressing each other by *ti* (the Croatian equivalent of German *Du*). To my great surprise, the hostess used this familial way too: such a trespass into privacy is hardly imaginable in a bus operating within Croatia. But is 'privacy' a relevant notion in a bus like this at all?

The longer the journey lasted, the more things seemed to pile up in the gangway; the less tidy it became. Things changed from being well-packed into a loose – and thus more voluminous – state. Food was taken out; people had home-made (or at least home-packed) meals with them. Saving money is one reason (the stops in Germany were long enough to be able to eat a full meal in the restaurants at the resting places, besides being hygiene halts), but food prepared by someone who cares provides the ones consuming it with a pleasant homely feeling, too. And so did the Turkish coffee – the only kind that could be bought on the bus.

Small transparent plastic bags for the rubbish were hanging on the armrests: a jolly installation as they moved to the rhythm of the road. The scent of mandarin orange peels was a counterpart to the smell from the toilet below.

Tiny 'private' spaces could be created only on, around and under the seats. Some young people had Walkmans to cut themselves off from the surroundings. I thought that reading would serve as a shield of privacy, but the persistent Croatian folk-pop music from the tape, the talking, singing, and too dim a light, proved it to be a rather inefficient kind of shield.

Sleeping next to strangers was mentioned above. But people do not feel like strangers after spending a night in such circumstances. 'We are in this together' is a shared feeling, I suppose. Gender is the last, basic differentiation category – people shift places according to their gender, but only if it is possible. Family members are privileged, for they can sleep next to each other more comfortably.

People were moving about in the bus, not only in need of the toilet or simply in need of movement (posing a question to the hostess was an 'excuse' for going to the lower part of the bus). 'Why don't you come and visit?' and 'Here I've come to visit you', was uttered rather often: people visited those they knew or the ones with whom they had made friends with at some of the stops. Others made space for them to sit down on the armrests, or they leaned on the seats while standing. Home-made schnaps brought from Croatia or Bosnia, beer and whisky bought along the way, were offered. The six hour ferry trip betwen Rostock and Trelleborg provided the opportunity for playing cards, treating friends or bus-acquaintances with coffee or beer, of sleeping and of sitting in pairs or small groups and talking.

'We'll be in luck – we just don't know if it will be good or bad!', a man said when we were entering Sweden again, hoping dearly that the police would not empty the bus in order to check what has been brought along, and thus delay us for another hour or two. We reached Malmö at 10 p.m.; he was proceeding to Gothenburg – another three and a half hours away – and had to be at work in his factory at 7 a.m. the next morning.

On reaching Slovenia, a fifteen-year-old girl telephoned her granny in Bosnia several times, informing her about how close to Zagreb we were getting. She seemed to know the exact schedule of the connections to the Bosnian town she was heading for. After sitting in the bus from Jönköping to Zagreb for thirty-three hours, she only had another six to go.

Time is a part of the value of travel. The 'time out' of the travel intensifies and extends subjective temporality. Or, travel functions to delay or interrupt the otherwise irrevocable passage of time (cf. Curtis and Pajaczkowska 1994:201). On a week's trip to Croatia, the stay is literally counted in hours. That is why the waiting at the state borders, i.e. treating people's time as worthless, is a particular form of humiliation (see Löfgren 1999:19, and esp. Haller 2000: 62, on queues as border measures that create most physical and psychological strain). People were angry when the wait at the German border made us miss the ferry to Sweden (we saw it leaving the harbour), but there was nothing we could do about it. The grey afternoon hours of waiting at a parking lot in Rostock harbour felt similar to the early morning hours I had spent looking at the dim landscape by the highway somewhere in Germany, just wanting the time to pass. Time out of time, the empty time of waiting, is a burden to be endured.

Borders and Communities

The relationship between *transnational* and *community* cannot be taken for granted; it has to be explored in each research situation. It is those links that transnationalism from below is really about. It is in the very practices of connecting distant places where transmigrant identities are entrenched.

I propose the existence of an *ad hoc community* of bus travellers. None of the passengers in any bus qualify for such a 'community';

the mere presence of people in a bus is not enough. It is rather obvious that 'ethnic' buses can be interpreted (and experienced) as being bits and pieces of real ethnic territories moving through Europe. The *ad hoc community* of bus travellers is thus 'place-bound' with regard to the very bus, yet created by people's interaction during the journey. The shared immediate bodily experiences, as well as the shared codes of behaviour and of wider (self)understanding, make it a community in spite of its 'on the road', highly contextual, and temporary character.

It does not make sense to simply assume that people are part of a community. 'It makes more sense to ask how it is that groups and communities are constituted as significant at different times and what the significance and participation of different people and practices in these processes implies' (Turner 2000:59). Such a complex question is able to capture the tension between the notion of identity as essential, fundamental, unitary and unchanging, and the notion that identities are constructed and reconstructed through action.

A reminder of the fact that migrants from the same country form heterogeneous groups of people, who came for different reasons and under different circumstances, with different personal and social endowments is never out of place. Ethnic groups in diaspora and exile are often seen as 'ethnic communities', but some intra-communal differences are visible even in the loose interaction patterns in the course of bus rides, and especially in more or less loudly uttered remarks intending a differentiation from within, a confirmation of self-ascribed distinction. 'Old' immigrants not only tend to see themselves as somewhat more refined and have more objections to the discomfort of the bus, in comparison to the people who came to Sweden as refugees in the 1990s (cf. Povrzanović Frykman 2001b). The former also seemed to be eager to point out their sharing of the Swedish living standards and standards of behaviour: the bus and the service were much better, many said, when the owner was a Swede. Some repeated rather loudly that that was the first and only time they were going to take that bus.

At the state borders, categorising on the basis of ascribed (national) belonging acquires an impersonal quality when everybody must show their passports at the same time. I believe that the interviews focusing on these moments would reveal a remarkable grass-roots expertise in the paradoxical nature of passports. The paradox lies in the fact that, while marking people as distinctive individuals, passports

> simultaneously constitute them as members of specific, horizontal collectivities and, in so doing, they underline that sustained possession of a distinctive individuality depends ultimately on the kind of collective legitimation that the state claims to embody (Rouse 1995:362).

Discussing 'the nationalization of anxiety' through 'the rituals and practices of border crossings', Orvar Löfgren (1999) offers a number of historical and recent examples of feelings of guilt and discrimination instilled at the borders. Löfgren stresses the striking role of the 'pedagogy of space' among the different ways of organising experiences, identities and communities.

Dieter Haller (2000) focuses on the community-organising aspect of the borders. He explains how the border between Spain and Gibraltar influences bodily experience which, mediated by local discourse, becomes a productive element in the habitualization of a Gibraltan national identity. Writing about people's narratives of controls, measures, queues, heat, and harassing experiences around the border crossing, Haller traces their experiences of uncertainty, insecurity, tension, stress, impotence and vulnerability.

Haller's interpretation strengthens my claim that the axiomatic understanding of identities as (always) being negotiated can hinder the perception of their imposed aspects. The cognitive approach reflected in 'believing' and 'imagining' communities has to be combined with the phenomenological approach of bodily 'feeling', bridging the gap between discourse and body. National identification cannot be fully understood if the habitualizing effects of national power on the bodies and emotions of individuals are not considered. Neither can the importance of arduous bodily experiences of people moving within transnational social fields.

Although their passport might be perceived as 'low-ranking' or suspicious by the pass-control representatives, people might re-confirm their emotional attachment to what the passport represents, and thereby enhance its symbolic value. I do not believe that any of my co-passengers despised, or was ashamed of, their passport at the moments of border police control. At least, one can presume that people, since forced to hold, look, and wait for their passports, engage in thinking about the meanings of their national belonging. It can be presumed that some emotions are raised in the process as well.

Haller (2000) explains how the stressful individual experiences of border crossing – communicated by the Gibraltarians as a part of their collective experience – generate a feeling of solidarity. In line with his explanation, it would be worth exploring what aspects of insideness and community people raise in their narration of the experiences of border crossings in the buses like the one described here. However, while collecting personal narratives is indispensable for getting to know something about people's own opinions, it is also necessary for the researcher to *be there*. The elliptic utterance, such as the one mentioned above, labelling the Austrian border police as *hajderovci* (Haider-supporters), might remain unrecorded in *post festum* personal narrations. No one commented upon it, and the theme was not developed further. However, that vengeful remark served to establish the sense of 'us', the people within the bus in relation to the 'they' of the police officers, who did not bother to greet the passengers, presumably because they did not see them as equals. The sense of 'us' established in that moment should be contextualised within the wider frames of frustrating experiences of discriminatory treatment, perceptions of difference and negotiations about 'belonging' to Europe (cf. Povrzanović Frykman 2002:143–149).

To illustrate my community-creating point, the similarities and the differences between the advertisement flyers can be mentioned, too, as printed by both the former Swedish and the actual Croatian owner of the same bus.

The only common traits are grammatical and spelling errors, and the fact that no web-sites or e-mail addresses are printed on either of the flyers – a fact worth noticing in Sweden, where most commodities are provided with Internet-addresses, not to mention all the possibilities of booking travels via the Internet. A potential passenger has to telephone and *talk* to the person responsible for reservations. (Tickets are sent home by post or collected and paid for in cash on the bus. They can be paid for in Sweden and collected on the bus by e.g. the relatives travelling from Croatia to Sweden. Saying the name is enough, no written confirmation is required.) Here another important community-invoking detail is striking: as when booking air flights though an 'ethnic' tourist office, or when reserving bus tickets, people are usually addressed by their first name – by *ti* (equivalent with German *Du*), and not by *vi* (German *Sie*), which in Croatian denotes a social distance in any formal contact.

The 'Swedish' flyer presents the bus – with several colour photographs of an atractive, blonde hostess – as a regular tourist charter line. The text is written in both languages, and accompanied by small Swedish and Croatian flags. (The Slovenian flag and the EU stars are also represented.) The professional image is confirmed by the facsimile of the company owner's signature.

The only (black-and-white) photograph on the 'Croatian' flyer shows the actual owner's face. Presented by first name only, he welcomes the passengers. Apart from a single line in Swedish, the the written information is entirely in Croatian. The text is minimal; mostly the flyer consists of the schedule and the price list. The white paper and the red details in the logo suggest the Croatian national colours, but perhaps they were just the cheapest variant. The target group is so obviously pre-defined that there is no need to flaunt national symbols.

Not only can 'ethnic' buses be interpreted as bits and pieces of ethnic territories moving through Europe, re-confirmed as such at international border controls. They might be experienced as such from the inside of the bus, too. The travel experience is shared with co-ethnics, which implies the exclusive use of mother-tongue and provides the most important grounds for community-feelings among people otherwise surrounded by and forced to use a foreign language. Further, the travellers 'feel at home' in sharing the codes of behaviour, and, not unimportantly, for the music accompanying much of the travel (regardless to their personal taste, it is familiar to them as a part of their wider cultural context).

Finally, the last stop is Zagreb, but the contract made with a local bus company makes it possible for the passengers from Sweden to reach other destinations within Croatia free of charge. Once reached, the national territory is equated with *home* in an important symbolic, but also practical, sense, which accentuates the physical moment of homecoming.[8]

Conclusion

During the mild evening of 6 January 2001, at the central bus station in Rijeka, the biggest Croatian Adriatic port, I witnessed the boarding of the buses leaving for Amsterdam, Basel and Frankfurt am Main. I could not see the luggage already stored in the buses, but I saw people in the gloomy cabin light, folding their coats and preparing for a long night. There were a lot more people around the buses. Last words, final hugs: Christmas was over, it was time to start working again.

A scene repeated all over the country, a standard sight. Large numbers make people and things more visible. The seeing off at the bus station in Rijeka was not purely individual and private; some kind of collectivity created by the tradition of migration as 'common destiny' had been confirmed. A part of national experience: ambivalence produced by dual attachments, by seeing clearly what is *better* at the other end of the transnational field – which always seems to be the place one is *not* occupying at the moment of consideration.

If this topic was to be explored further, a more encompassing comparative ethnography of situational relations among the transnational travellers would be required, of travelling to other destinations and by different means of transportation. Community-producing moments during the bus ride itself would be related to the subsequent narration about the journeys. A collection of personal narratives on those bus rides, compared to the narratives of people staying behind, would be a precondition for more complex insights.

The aim of this article, however, is limited to suggesting the explanatory potentials of micro-ethnographic studies of transnational practices such as travelling back and forth. Such studies can provide insights that are lacking in interpretations of ethnic and national identifications as processes of negotiation. They can namely hinder the perception of their imposed aspects.

Identities 'are not free-floating, they are limited by borders and boundaries' (Sarup 1994:95). We need to know what is going on from the perspective of people who experience these limits. The metaphor of 'border crossing' often seems to imply the ease of movement and the disruption of relations between place and identity. If seen against the background of experiences attainable through fieldwork, the border crossings might appear as being shadowed by imposed identities.

Togetherness as an outcome of shared bodily experiences is important not only in situations of extreme hardship, but also in 'trivial' situations such as a twenty-six-hour bus ride. The shared bodily experiences of physical proximity and restrictions, uneasiness and pain, of controlled movement and exposure to the power of state authorities on different borders, are cohesion-producing forces. Although temporary and not a basis for further social intercourse of the very individuals gathered in the bus, their travels do affect much larger groups of people at both (or all) sides of transnational social fields. They may not be formative experiences, but they add to people's self-understanding in terms of belonging to an ethnic or national group. Thus, ethnographic insights in such experiences add to the understanding of how transnationalism, 'far from erasing the local identifications and meaning systems, actually relies on them to sustain transnational ties' (Guarnizo and Smith 1998:15).

The embodied geography of physical distances and national borders is just one element of transnational individuals' and groups' identification processes. Nevertheless, it is central to ethnographic accounts on the multiple and often burdensome experiences of connecting places.

Notes

*   This essay is a considerably shortened and partially rewritten version of the article 'Connecting Places, Enduring the Distance: Transnationalism as a Bodily Experience' published in *Ethnologia Scandinavica* vol. 31, 2001. The article was written in the context of my work on the project entitled 'Seeds of War: Narrative Construction of Identities in Diaspora and Exile', financed by the Swedish

Council for Research in the Humanities and Social Sciences (HSFR) in 2000 and 2001 (presented in Povrzanović Frykman 2001b).

1   'These spaces denote dynamic processes, not static notions of ties and position. Cultural, political, and economic processes in transnational social spaces involve the accumulation, use, and effects of various sorts of capital, their volume and convertibility: economic capital, human capital, such as educational credentials, skills and know-how, and social capital, mainly resources inherent in or transmitted through social and symbolic ties' (Faist 2000:200).

2   By mentioning it first, I am pointing out the fact that 'phoning still is the most democratic, the most accessible and the most widely used entry to transnational social fields – from both (or all) sides. Yet, the simple example of the accessibility of this – oldest – technology enabling direct communication and defeating physical distance, may remind us of the manifold inequalities constitutive of *transnationalism from below*. Considered from e.g. a Swedish perspective where large parts of the population have access to the Internet at home, it might be easily forgotten that the wide everyday use of the telephone is the latest novelty in many localities from which labour migrants and refugees originate. For example, in a region some 60 km south-west of Zagreb, people living in the villages some 10 km from the local centre, were connected to the Croatian telecommunication system only in the late 1990s, at high private expense. These were often paid for by the money earned by their children and relatives in Austria and Germany.

3   In contrast to that, the airport of Brnik, Ljubljana, as well as the check-in counters at Kastrup, Copenhagen, are becoming true 'Yugoslav' places a couple of times a week, always at very late or very early hours: they might be the only remaining places where all south-eastern European languages can be heard at the same time. So far, the Slovene national air-company is offering the only direct connection from Copenhagen, which happens also to be cheaper than any other air-connection to destinations within the former Yugoslav space. So, people from all parts of former Yugoslavia use it, and continue their journey from Ljubljana.

4   According to the figures from *The Croatian Statistics Yearbook* for 1995, 53.39% of ethnic Croats live in Croatia, 13.95% in other countries – successors of former Yugoslavia, and some 11.86% live in other (mostly Western) European countries 20.80% live on all other continents. Most of those in Western Europe (6.43%) live in Germany. Some 30,000 Croats (0.43% of ethnic Croats worldwide) live in Sweden.

5   Luis E. Guarnizo and Michael P. Smith (1998:5–6) explain that 'given the declining political influence of working-class movements in the face of the global reorganization of capitalism, all sorts of new social actors on the transnational stage are now being invested with oppositional possibilities, despite the fact that their practices are neither self-consciously resistant nor even loosely political in character. ... While transnational practices and hybrid identities are indeed potentially counter-hegemonic, they are by no means always resistant. ... [T]he liminal sites of transnational practices and discourses can be used for the purposes of capital accumulation quite as effectively as for the purpose of contesting hegemonic narratives of race, ethnicity, class, and nation'.

6   Such meanings are importantly related to tourism as the 'most profoundly privi-
     leged and subjective form of modern travel ... one of the principal symbolic
     experiences available to the modern self. The imperative to travel signifies the
     quest for the acquisition of knowledge and desire to return to a utopian space
     of freedom, abundance and transparency. Psychic desires are displaced in partial
     and vicarious participation in another set of relations (another place and time),
     and the self becomes realised as the hero of its own narrative of departure and
     return' (Robertson et al. 1994:5).

7   I answered personal questions straightforwardly. It was in the area of personal
     information that my difference from 'standard bus traveller' was soon noticed.
     I was different because of being an academic, and for not belonging to either of
     the groups equally represented on the bus – of people who came to Sweden as
     refugees in the 1990s, or of Croatian labour migrants who came to Sweden in
     the 1960s. No private or otherwise delicate issues are touched upon in this text.
     Everyone – even the bus – is kept anonymous (I did not ask for people's names
     anyway). I met three people on the bus whom I knew from before. The conver-
     sations I had with them, on matters other than those concerning transnational
     travel, are not included in this text.

8   At the very beginning of the journey to Croatia, the hostess made a statement
     that at first seemed to be a slip of a tongue, but which, indeed, confirmed the
     transmigrant character of these bus rides. She namely told the passengers with
     open return tickets that they would have to make the reservation ten days before
     'going home' – to Sweden. Otherwise, the mention of 'home' was always with
     reference to people's homes in Croatia and Bosnia-Hercegovina (although for
     many it literally meant only their relatives' homes).

References

Amit-Talai, Vered 1998: Risky Hiatuses and the Limits of Social Imagination: Expatriacy
   in the Cayman Islands. In *Migrants of Identity: Perceptions of Home in a World of Movement*, ed. Nigel Rapport and Andrew Dawson, 41–59. Oxford, New York: Berg.
Chambers, Ian 1994: *Migrancy, Culture, Identity*. London and New York: Routledge.
Csordas, Thomas J. 1994: Introduction: The Body as Representation and Being-in-
   the-World. In *Embodiment and Experience: The Existential Ground of Culture and
   Self*, ed. Thomas J. Csordas, 1–24. Cambridge: Cambridge University Press.
Curtis, Barry, and Pajaczkowska, Claire 1994: 'Getting There': Travel, Time and Nar-
   rative. In *Travellers' Tales: Narratives of home and displacement*, George Robertson
   et al. (eds), 199–215. London and New York: Routledge.
Faist, Thomas 2000: *The Volume and Dynamics of International Migration and Transnational Social Spaces*. Oxford: Clarendon Press.
Guarnizo, Luis Eduardo and Smith, Michael 1998: The Locations of Transnationalism.
   In *Transnationalism from Below*, Michael Peter Smith and Luis Eduardo Guarnizo
   (eds), 3–34. New Brunswick and London: Transaction Publishers.
Haller, Dieter 2000: The Smuggler and the Beauty Queen. The Border and Sovereignty
   as Sources of Body Style in Gibraltar. *Ethnologia Europaea* 30(2): 57–72.

Jackson, Michael 1983: Knowledge of the Body. *Man* (N.S.) 18: 327–345.

Kearney, Michael 1991: Borders and Boundaries of State and Self at the End of Empire. *Journal of Historical Sociology* 4(1): 52–74.

Löfgren, Orvar 1999: Crossing Borders. The Nationalization of Anxiety. *Ethnologia Scandinavica* 29: 3–27.

Marcus, George 1995: Ethnography In/Of the World System: The Emergence of Multi-Sited Ethnography. *Annual Review of Anthropology* 24: 95–117.

Portes, Alejandro, Guarnizo, Luis E., and Landolt, Patricia 1999: The Study of Transnationalism: Pitfalls and Promise of an Emergent Research Field. *Ethnic and Racial Studies* 22(2): 217–237.

Povrzanović, Maja 1997. Identities in War: Embodiments of Violence and Places of Belonging. *Ethnologia Europaea* 27(2): 153–162.

Povrzanović Frykman, Maja 2001a: Challenges of Belonging in Diaspora and Exile: an Introduction. In *Beyond Integration: Challenges of Belonging in Diaspora and Exile*, Maja Povrzanović Frykman (ed.), 11–40. Lund: Nordic Academic Press.

Povrzanović Frykman, Maja 2001b: Construction of Identities in Diaspora and Exile: Croats in Sweden in the 1990s. In *Beyond Integration: Challenges of Belonging in Diaspora and Exile*, Maja Povrzanović Frykman (ed.), 166–194. Lund: Nordic Academic Press.

Povrzanović Frykman, Maja 2002: Establishing and Dissolving Cultural Boundaries: *Croatian Culture* in Diasporic Contexts. In *The Balkans in Focus: Cultural Boundaries in Europe*, Sanimir Resic and Barbara Törnquist-Plewa (eds), 137–188. Lund: Nordic Academic Press.

Robertson, George, et al. 1994: As the World Turns: Introduction. In *Travellers' Tales: Narratives of Home and Displacement*, George Robertson, Melinda Mash, Lisa Tickner, Jon Bird, Barry Curtis and Tim Putnam (eds), 1–6. London and New York: Routledge.

Rouse, Roger 1995: Questions of Identity: Personhood and Collectivity in Transnational Migration to the United States. *Critique of Anthropology* 15(4): 351–380.

Sarup, Madan 1994: Home and Identity. In *Travellers' Tales: Narratives of home and displacement*, George Robertson et al. (eds), 93–104. London and New York: Routledge.

Turner, Aaron 2000: Embodied Ethnography: Doing Culture. *Social Anthropology* 8(1): 51–60.

GHASSAN HAGE

The Differential Intensities of Social Reality

Migration, Participation and Guilt

Introduction

In *Sentiments Filiaux d'un Parricide*, Proust refers to what he quali-fies as 'the abominable, voluptuous act called 'reading the paper'.' Here was a practice, Proust writes, 'whereby all the misfortunes and cataclysms suffered by the universe in the last twenty-four hours' from 'battles which have cost the lives of fifty thousand men', to murders, bankruptcies and divorces, are all 'transmuted into a morning feast for our personal entertainment', making 'an excel-lent and particularly bracing accompaniment to a few mouthfuls of *café au lait*'. Commenting on this text, Bourdieu sees it as the 'the aesthete's variant' of the practice of reading the newspaper. He calls for a more differentiated analysis of this 'mediated, relatively abstract experience of the social world supplied by newspaper read-ing'. He points out that the nature of this reading will vary, for example, as a function of variations in physical space depending, that is, on whether the item is a piece of local news or interna-tional news. It will also depend on variations in social distance, such as differences in the degree of political commitment, 'from the detachment depicted in Proust's text to the activist's outrage or enthusiasm'.[1]

Unsurprisingly, in the research I have been conducting on expe-riences of nostalgia and homesickness among Sydney's Lebanese community, the practice of reading/listening to/watching the news about 'the homeland' has emerged as an important element in

Lebanese everyday life. It was something people yearned for and awaited, sometimes with great excitement. It was also an important trigger of sometimes implicit, but sometimes also explicit, intense and visible feelings of nostalgia. Most importantly, as I will detail below, consuming news about Lebanon is hardly ever a passive experience for most first generation Lebanese migrants. Clearly, no Lebanese I have encountered read the news about Lebanon as 'entertainment' with either their *café au lait* or the *ahwheh* (Lebanese coffee) ritualistically enjoyed with the 'home news'.

Lebanese people were clearly affected by the news, but just as clearly, people were affected by it *in various ways, and to differing degrees*. It is in this context that the pertinence of Bourdieu's comments became particularly clear to me. Here was 'news' from which people were equally distant as far as the physical Sydney–Beirut distance was concerned, but were clearly unequally 'distant' as far as the social distance that separated them from it was concerned. They were differentially *implicated* by it and experienced it with varying *intensities*.[2]

It is these two related ideas of the differential modes of being implicated by the news and the related intensity with which one experiences the news in which one is implicated that I want to reflect on here.[3] I want to deploy these two notions of implication and intensity as analytical tools for measuring one's affective and symbolic 'distance' from the news. This conceptualisation of affective and symbolic distance is clearly an important aspect of any research on nostalgia and its place in migrant cultures, I also think that it can open a new field of investigation into an aspect of social life that we all encounter and which nevertheless remains highly under-researched or commented on, and that is 'the intensity of reality' in general. We all go through our daily lives knowing and/or feeling that some things leave in and on us a much deeper impression than others, that certain realities are experienced more intensely than others. Intensity as I will use it here is not primarily physical, although it is also that. It is primarily affective. An intensely experienced reality is not the same as a 'hard hitting' reality. Intensity has more to do with the extent to which a reality is involving and affecting. The effect of a machine or a city street can be very strong on a migrant worker from a rural background, but we cannot say that she necessarily experiences them intensively just because of their strong physical effect. An intense reality is primarily an intense *relation* where the person's engagement in reality contributes to constructing its intensity. How we can capture this analytically, and how we can explain it, seems to me an important question. While I will confine myself here to some preliminary reflections on how to think the way this intensity is experienced in the process of reading the news, I will attempt to conclude by commenting on the possibilities of investigating this question in other areas of social life.

Lebanese News and News about Lebanon

News of family and friends, and of the political situation in Lebanon are essential elements in sustaining the lives of those Australian Lebanese still affectively, socially and sometimes economically connected to Lebanon (which of course does not encompass all Australian Lebanese). The information received is comforting in that it sustains the feeling that people have not totally left their home country, are still connected to it, and feel implicated by what is happening in it. News items are subjects of discussion and sometimes of intense arguments and operate as classical triggers of nostalgic feelings.

As is always the case, while personal and local news of kin and friends are communicated in personal correspondence, news about the political situation and other general social issues are mainly communicated by the media.[4] Although there are a number of radio stations that people listen to frequently, and various televisually communicated news in Arabic, my research has been chiefly concerned with the printed media.

There are three types of newspaper from which news about Lebanon can be obtained: the mainstream Australian newspapers, the Australian Lebanese newspapers and the Lebanese newspapers printed in Lebanon. These need to be differentiated not only because of the different news they communicate but because each type of newspapers has in itself a different implicating effect on the person reading it. In the very nature of the newspaper one can already perceive different modes of 'feeling' and experiencing the news.

News items about Lebanon consumed in the mainstream Australian newspapers, for example, are often experienced as alienating, even when because of a scarcity of information they are welcome. Such items are typically in the 'world section' of the newspaper. They are clearly intended for non-Lebanese. The very mode of reporting them is a reporting by non-Lebanese for non-Lebanese. The fact that this news is communicated in English on a page where many other items of world news are printed situates the reader in Australia, emphasising the distance between the reader and the event being reported. Complaints by the Lebanese such as 'they only have a news item on Lebanon when there is a bomb', or, 'since the war ended Lebanon has become less interesting for them' are often part of the endless politics of recognition which structures the migrant's presence in the host society. Thus a question such as, 'did you see the article on Lebanon in the *Sydney Morning Herald*' is less an urging to read such news for its content and more a celebration of a moment of recognition by the dominant culture. This, in itself, implicates the Lebanese reader in the Australian rather than Lebanese culture, increasing the distancing effect of the news item.

News items in the Australian Lebanese paper work differently. They operate metonymically as a fragment of an imaginary Lebanon and as such bring one closer to the event that is being reported. The use of the Arabic language and the assumed knowledge of certain basics (there are no distancing statements such as 'Prime Minister Hariri, the wealthy businessman who has been in power since…' which one finds in non-Lebanese newspapers) work to create a feeling of continuity between the event and its reporting and a feeling of community between the reported event and the reader. Increasingly, the news in the Australian Lebanese newspaper is nothing other than the reproduction, under a special agreement, and sometimes on the same day it appears in Lebanon, of a news text produced in Lebanon by one of the Lebanese dailies.

Despite the above, however, the Lebanese in Australia express a clear preference to reading the same text from the original Lebanese paper that produced it. This is due to the nature of the totality of the newspaper as a collection of texts and brings us to an important aspect of reading.

What makes the same news item more popular in its 'original' setting is clearly the textual context in which it is present, that is, the totality of the other items that are published with it in the newspaper. While the article in the Lebanese Australian paper can be the same as the one in the Lebanese paper, next to it may be news items, ads, announcements which give the article itself a sometimes radically different relation to the event it is reporting. Thus, while an article might be appearing in a Lebanese Australian paper straight from the Lebanese press in Beirut, the fact that next to it is an ad for a bakery in Campsie and an article about an Australian-Lebanese Liberal Party fund-raiser in Melbourne makes the news more Australian. It again creates a certain 'distancing effect', or even an unwelcome intrusion of the reality of migration to the scene of reading that the Lebanese migrant might be trying to escape by immersing himself or herself in the Lebanese news.

This is why despite the availability of a constant flow of information, a person arriving from Lebanon is often quickly asked for the Lebanese paper even if the news in it is usually two or three days old. The reading of a news item in the Lebanese paper is a totally Lebanese experience where belonging to the Australian physical space becomes immaterial and suspended. The Lebanese newspaper does not just offer a genuinely Lebanese perspective on a topic; the newspaper positions the reader in Lebanon. As one is reading about the events of the day on page 1, next to it is an ad for a home decoration expo in Beirut. You can even read about what is happening in Australia as perceived in/from Lebanon. Thus, if the news item in the Lebanese Australian paper works metonymically to bridge the distance between 'Lebanon' as an imagined totality and the migrant, the Lebanese paper works metaphorically (in that the totality of the relations between the different articles in it become a metaphor for the totality of the relations that constitute Lebanon as an imaginary nation).

This is why the Lebanese newspaper provides an imaginary positioning of the self as a Lebanese in Lebanon, not as a Lebanese migrant in Australia reading about Lebanon. One manages to experience what Anderson talks about as unisonnance at a distance.[5] You share *the* 'national' perspective and in the process the distance between the report and the news event is almost abolished. In reading the newspaper, one does not read about the nation, one reads the nation.

What is clear from the above is that when reading a newspaper article, one does not just relate to the article being read. Readers at every moment are reading the whole newspaper as a system of relations between different news items, ads, announcements, etc… This system of relations, as I have suggested, already positions the reader at a specific distance from the reported events and allows (but does not necessitate) him or her to experience them with greater intensity, depending on the extent of the investment one has in such events.

Thus, just because the distance from the event allowed by specific newspapers allows them to be experienced with specific intensities, this does not mean that the reader passively accepts whatever intensity is communicated by the newspaper. In the following section, I want to examine how readers are themselves capable of relating to news items in specific ways so as to vary their intensity. This is what I will call strategies of intensification.

Strategies of Intensification

Let me begin with two short ethnographic accounts.

> I am watching Maurice reading the paper. He is sitting on a chair behind the counter of his dry cleaning business. His business is located on the ground floor of his family house in Dulwich Hill, Sydney.
>
> For the last hour, every time there have been no customers around he has pulled the Australian Lebanese paper from underneath the counter and reads. He knows I am 'studying his family'. We are distantly related and he has become used to me sitting in the corner of his shop reading a book or scribbling in my notebook. He migrated to Australia twelve years ago from a village in North Lebanon. He married a woman from the same village in Australia

ten years ago. When he first settled in Sydney, he worked for Australia Post. He bought the business the same year he married. He thinks the business is 'slow' but he has been saying this ever since he bought it. Nevertheless, he is clearly not doing very well economically. His lifestyle does not allow him to put his kids in a Catholic school as he would have liked.

Sometimes Maurice gets to read the paper for one minute, sometimes for two or three. This time it has been more than five minutes since a customer came and he has become quite absorbed in his reading. He was also becoming visibly agitated, moving nervously on his stool.

'*Yeh'rek deenak akhroot!*' he mutters. He slaps the paper with the back of his hand. '*Eh akeed! lahwayne baddak trooh? 'a Sooriyya!*. '*Tfehh 'alayk shoo wahtee*'. He looks at me. 'Lebanon is finished', he tells me in Arabic. 'If I was in Lebanon I would spit on every single politician.' 'Put this in your study', he jokes. Maurice was reading about the Lebanese Prime Minister going to Syria to consult with the Syrian government about the coming Lebanese elections. Like many Maronites, he resents the way, since the civil war has ended, Lebanese politicians have become dependent on Syria for the running of Lebanese affairs. His comments take the form of a direct conversation with the Prime Minister: 'Of course! Where else you're gonna go? To Syria! Shame on you, you lowly thing.'

Since beginning this research, I have become quite interested with the mutterings and the bodily movements that accompanied newspaper readings. Maurice's comments and particularly the act of slapping the paper with the back of the hand were quite common. But before analysing these movements it is useful to give another short ethnographic account.

It is lunch-time on Sunday. Maurice's brother, Lucien, a reasonably successful businessman, is visiting, and so is Maurice's Lebanese next-door neighbour, Raymond, who runs the corner store. Both have come with their families. The lunch is almost a ritual, with the same people gathering in Maurice's backyard on a monthly and sometimes a fortnightly basis.

After lunch, Maurice is sitting on the lunch table having a coffee and reading the Australian Lebanese paper. Others are also having coffee, chatting to each other or playing with kids. Maurice starts muttering '*Yeh'rek deenak akhroot!* (Damn you!). He turns to Raymond:

– Did you read this!? It says that Assad (Syria's president) expressed to Hraoui (Lebanon's president) his displeasure with the in-fighting within the government. And now where is Hariri gone? '*a Sooriyya*!!

Lucien's wife, Amal, looks smilingly at Maurice and says:

– I don't know why you get so worked up about it. They obviously can't govern on their own. Maybe we should be thankful that the Syrians are intervening, otherwise they'll spend their time fighting each other and nothing gets done.

– Listen to her! Maurice exclaims. Well, why doesn't Assad declare himself the president of Lebanon and forget about this masquerade.

Raymond nods in agreement:

– This way it will become clear who is ruling us. Maybe then people will wake up to what is happening and start resisting.

Lucien shakes his head:

– You're eager for a new war, are you?

– Anything is better than this…

– Maybe you've forgotten what it was like.

Maurice folds the newspaper and slaps it on the table.

– Oh you get off it Lucien! You don't really care any more what happens there. What was it like? It was better than what it has become like now. Everyone is getting poor, now, and the Syrians are stealing everything.

– I'd rather fight than allow this situation to go on, agreed Raymond. At least, we need to get rid of this lousy government.

– If I was in Lebanon, I would spit on them one by one, exclaimed Maurice.

In examining the above argument, which happened almost two months after the first, I was struck by the almost exact similarity of Maurice's utterings on the two occasions. In a sense, it was irrelevant whether he was talking to himself or 'having an argument'. Or, to put it differently, we can say that the argument was merely a means for Maurice to say what he wanted to say.

Lebanese Australians discussing news events about Lebanon hardly ever discuss them with people from 'the opposite side' of the Lebanese religious or political divide. Most arguments, such as the above, are what discourse analysts refer to as pseudo-arguments. In the light of the above, I want to suggest that arguing over the news is like slapping the paper, slapping it on the table, shouting at it, etc… They all constitute part of a whole series of utterances, interactions and bodily movements which can be referred to as strategies of intensification: strategies aimed at narrowing the physical and symbolic gap between the news event and the reader, and in the process augmenting the intensity of this reality for that reader.

As I have already suggested, this wish to intensify reality is motivated by a desire to be more implicated by the news/event. To be implicated in an event, is to develop a sense of involvement in it, of being part of its unfolding. At one level, in the above, one might think that the reason for wanting to be implicated in such a way is evident: Lebanese migrants feel 'distant' from events occurring in Lebanon and their strategies of intensification are part of a wider range of strategies in which they try to deal with this distance and with their 'homesickness'. This is clearly demonstrated in Maurice's direct expression of such a desire for proximity: 'if I was in Lebanon…', and in the way he turns his comments about the Prime Minister into a direct conversational mode as if he was right 'there' with him. But why do such Lebanese want to be more implicated? Such a desire cannot be taken for granted, or, more importantly, such a desire cannot be taken to be equally felt among all Lebanese migrants.

Indeed, as the 'argument' reported above clearly shows, what differentiated the two 'opposing parties', Lucien and Amal, and the rest, is precisely an unequal wish to intensify the news event and be implicated by it. This is evident from the degree of affect, and one is tempted to say 'objectivity', characterising the statements of each side. Lucien and Amal's comments appear far more reasonable and detached than the highly charged 'let's have a war again' discourse of the others. Maurice's comments and mutterings are infused with affect made clear by his very bodily demeanour while interacting with the news item. It is also made clear by his choice of words, his swearing and his metaphors ('damn you!', 'I would spit on them'). Maurice's exclamation to his brother reveals to us what is perceived to be at stake throughout the process of intensification: 'You don't really care any more what happens there', he tells him.

For the person engaging in the process of intensification, the wish to be affectively implicated by the news event is perceived as the result of caring. It is thinking that what is happening is important and is worthwhile being part of. It is possessing what Bourdieu calls the *illusio*.[6] In the context of the highly conflictual space of Lebanese politics which demand of you to take the side of your community, detached observations become constructed by Maurice as 'not caring'.

There is a subjective relation established therefore between various elements we have mentioned above: caring, being part of, *illusio*, being implicated, intensity of reality. To care about a reality is to share in the *illusio* that it is worthwhile being part of it or being implicated in it, and the more one becomes implicated in a reality the more one feels it intensely. This is, at least, how the wish to be more implicated by the news is experienced by those intensifying it. The question we have asked, however, remains to be answered: why do some people care and want such an intensity more than others? To answer this question takes us into the territory of social belonging which is yet another concept on the same wave length as 'being part of', 'being implicated', etc.

Migration, Guilt and the State of the Debt – Towards a Moral Economy of Social Belonging

One of the most important theories that link up the degrees of being implicated by reality with the intensity of this reality is Marx's theory of alienation. Marx conceives humans' implication in social reality in general along the model of, and as causally related to, their implication in the process of production. For participation in society to be a genuine participation, that is for it to generate for the participant a feeling that they are part of society and implicated by it, the participant has to feel that they are in control over the process of production (not only of goods, but also of the total social reality encompassed by the production process). Among its many important facets, Marx's theory of alienation is precisely a theorisation of the way the lack of control over the process of production leads the social reality to become less *intensely* experienced by the worker. This diminishing of the intensity of reality is one of the fundamental meanings of estrangement. Marx, that is to say already understood that reality was not experienced by all with the same intensity. And intensity was not for him a question of how hard-hitting capitalist machinery was, for example, but of how implicating it was: the degree to which the worker related to it affectively as part of what constitutes his or her being. To a certain extent, Marx posited a normative intensity which he saw as particular to human beings, and argued that capitalism leads to a dehumanising relation to reality, such that humans stop experiencing it with the intensity they ought to be able to experience it with.

Notwithstanding the importance of this production-based understanding of the nature of one's implication in social reality, I would like to propose that there is also another important exchange-based understanding of which the components can be found in the anthropological theorisation of gift exchange.

In *The Genealogy of Morals*, Nietzsche comments that:

> the community, too, stands to its members in that same vital basic relation, that of the creditor to his debtors. One lives in a community, one enjoys the advantages of a communality (oh what advantages! We sometimes underrate them today), one dwells protected, cared for, in peace and trustfulness, without fear of certain injuries and hostile acts to which the man *outside*, the 'man without peace,' is exposed–a German will understand the original connotations of *Elend*–since one has bound and pledged oneself to the community precisely with a view to injuries and hostile acts. What will happen *if this pledge is broken*? The community, the disappointed creditor, will get what repayment it can, one may depend on that.[7]

Communal life, one can read Nietzsche as saying, is a gift that the community expect those who receive it to reciprocate. In certain forms of Catholicism, the life of an individual itself is perceived as a gift from God. Consequently, such Catholic individuals will see their lives as marked by an original guilt associated with their state of indebtedness to God. Most importantly for us, they conceive of living in a religious manner, that is, of religiously guided participation in life, as a mode of repaying the debt. To be *religiously implicated* in life is the mode of repaying the religious debt.

In much the same way, Nietzsche is pointing out that social/communal life is also perceived as a gift. If God gives us the gift of life as such, it is our community that gives us the gift of social life. And if in being religiously implicated one repays the gift of life, it is in being socially and communally implicated that one repays the gift of social life. Being a family member is a gift from the family. Being a national is a gift from the nation. One repays this gift through a life-long participation in the family and community or whichever communal group individuals feel has provided them with that gift of communality. The sublime element of dying for one's nation must partly lie in the debt-free state nationalist martyrs acquire in this process: the nation gave them the gift of life and they gave their life back to the nation. Generally however, one remains in the debt of the community, repaying it in slow instalments through a life-time of participating in it.

We can see from the above why migration can be a guilt-inducing process. To leave the communal group to which one is indebted is precisely to refrain from repaying the debt. It is important to re-member that there is no necessary communal entity we feel indebted to. Not all migrants feel indebted to their nation, for example, but most will feel indebted to their family. This guilt-inducing state of indebtedness is most apparent in times of crisis when your fam-ily, your village or your nation is going through a hard time and you (the subject organically related to the community through the original debt of social/communal life) are not there to help. When you do not share the fate of the collectivity which gave you social life you are guilty of letting others pay alone for a debt you are collectively responsible for.

I think that it is in the above that the *desire* to be implicated, to intensify reality among Lebanese migrants has to be located. Strategies of intensification are guilt-ridden moves within a general moral economy of social belonging. That is why they are permeated by an affective language. They are modes of repayment: the more intense the mode of being implicated, the more 'debt' one repays in this symbolic-moral economy.

So far in the above, in order to emphasise the process I was introducing, I have drawn a picture of what can be called an elementary form of social indebtedness: one community member indebted to one community. The empirical situation which each individual finds themself in is clearly far more complicated than this. Most importantly, feelings of indebtedness are not restricted to one communal formation. One can belong with equal or varying intensity to several communities. Furthermore, the gift of social life is not offered to individuals only in the process of being born in a specific community. One can incur the debt of communality by voluntarily becoming part of a community that accepts one in its midst. This, of course, can be the case in the process of migration, to which I want to return now.

If migrants leave their original community in a state of debt and with guilt-ridden feelings of having left without repaying the debt, no sooner do they settle in a new country than they incur a new debt. If the new country does not offer originally the same sense of communality one finds in the home country, it nevertheless offers hopes of a better of future which is an important ingredient in any kind of life. This creates a complex situation where, while the participation in the host community can be seen as repayment of the debt of belonging to it, this same participation can accentuate feelings of guilt towards the original community. Thus, it is not uncommon for migrants, especially in the early stages of migrations, to refrain from showing an excessive enthusiasm towards the host country in front of their 'original' countrymen and women, even if they genuinely feel excited about the social and economic opportunities it is offering them. Such enthusiasm can be constructed as a form of social treason: a sign that one has forgotten about one's original debt.

Matters are complicated further by the fact that the development of a moral obligation towards a country which has offered you the gift of a new life is also linked to *how* this gift is offered. Here the whole subtlety of gift exchange comes to the fore. The gifts that create the greatest moral obligations are the gifts that are offered most graciously. If the one who offers the gift keeps reminding one of their state of indebtedness or if the gift is given ungraciously, than the moral obligation, while always present, becomes nevertheless less morally obliging. Thus, comments such as 'they treated us like beggars' by Lebanese migrants who have nevertheless received an Australian entry visa imply a gift that is badly offered (by the Australian embassy!). Here the whole politics of a country's immigration policies and how its national discourse constructs migrants becomes implicated in this moral economy. It is interesting how the more a country hardens its immigration policy and 'treats its migrants like beggars', the more the discourses demanding migrant adhesion to the nation abound, betraying an implicit recognition or fear that the way the offer of a new life is made does not carry with it the moral obligation of adhesion.

To conclude these reflections, I would like to mention an important factor determining the state of indebtedness, though by no means the last one, and that is the degree of social and economic success one experiences in the host country. The feelings of satisfaction generated from a sense that one has achieved something in the process of migration is also a sense of how much the host country has offered and is clearly of great importance in determining the relation of indebtedness with it. It is noteworthy in the case of the 'argument' we have examined above that Maurice's brother and his wife were far more successful economically than he or his neighbour were. To a certain extent one can say that excessive attachment to one's original country is a strategy of compensation for one's life not turning out as hoped for.

Notes

1   Pierre Bourdieu, *Distinction: A Social Critique of the Judgement of Taste*, London, Melbourne and Henley: Routledge and Kegan Paul, 1984, p. 21.

2   I have borrowed the concept of 'being implicated by the news' from the work of

Ken Wark, *Virtual Geographies*, Bloomington and Indianapolis, Indiana University Press, 1997, where he talks of the implicating capacity of the 'media vector', the vector of informational flow. For Wark, the media vector has an inherently implicating capacity. Without disagreeing with this, my aim is to develop the idea that these vectors are also vectors of affect and that there are degrees of implications based on their mode of reception. This does not only mean that people are differentially affected by the inherent implicating capacity of the vector, but that subjects often *seek* in different ways to be implicated by the vector.

3   I do not differentiate here between the experience of news about a place and a lived experience of the place itself. For my purpose both are part of the subject's social reality, albeit in different ways.

4   Since the war, this is referred to in colloquial Lebanese as *al-haleh* . This generally means: 'the situation'. Thus, *keef al-haleh?* (what's 'the situation' like?) embodies a request for news about how peaceful 'the situation' in the country is.

5   Benedict Anderson, *Imagined Communities: Reflections on the Origins and Spread of Nationalism*, London: Verso Press, 1983.

6   Pierre Bourdieu, *The Logic of Practice*, Oxford: Polity Press, 1990, pp: 66–67.

7   Friedrich Nietzsche, Genealogy of morals, in Walter Kaufmann (ed), *Basic Writng of Nietzsche*, New York: the Modern Library, 1992, p. 507.

References

Anderson, Benedict 1983: *Imagined Communities: Reflections on the Origins and Spread of Nationalism*, London: Verso Press.

Pierre Bourdieu 1984, *Distinction: A Social Critique of the Judgement of Taste*, London, Melbourne and Henley: Routledge and Kegan Paul.

Bourdieu, Pierre 1990: *The Logic of Practice*, Oxford: Polity Press, 1990.

Friedrich Nietzsche, Genealogy of morals, in Walter Kaufmann (ed) 1992: *Basic Writings of Nietzsche*, New York: the Modern Library.

Wark, Ken 1997, *Virtual Geographies*, Bloomington and Indianapolis: Indiana University Press.

MICHAEL JACKSON

The Politics of Reconciliation

Reflections on Postwar Sierra Leone

> And might it not be … that we also have appointments to keep in the past, in what has gone before and is for the most part extinguished, and must go there in search of places and people who have some connection with us on the far side of time, so to speak?
>
> W.G. Sebald, *Austerlitz,* p.360

I had not been in Sierra Leone for more than ten years, and when I returned in January 2002 the war was just ending. Signs of a new dispensation were everywhere. At the airport, a placard in the old hangar that served as an Arrivals hall read Under Rehabilitation, reassuring you that this noisy, dismal shed was only a momentary inconvenience. Welcome to Sierra Leone, said the hoarding outside, If you cannot help us, please do not corrupt us. Downtown, in the crowded streets, there were poda-podas called Better Days Are Coming, Human Right, and O Life at Last. A fishing boat on Lumley beach had been named Democracy. Young men were wearing T-shirts, saying Forgive and Reconcile for National Development. And everywhere there were vehicles and offices belonging to NGOs and UN agencies, with Reconstruction, Rehabilitation, Reconciliation, and Resettlement the recurring words. One could not help but be affected by this ostensible spirit of renewal. But how realistic was it? The foreign aid. The disarmament process one read about in the daily papers. The Truth and Reconciliation Commission that was beginning its work. Was not this language of reconciliation a little like the language of human rights, I wondered, at once too abstract and too Eurocentric? A moral order imposed by the north upon the south, and as such, simply a new variation of the old self-extolling theme of the white man's burden?

A couple of days after arriving back in Freetown I was stuck in traffic. Ahead of me, a large truck, attempting to pass between the lines of parked and gridlocked cars had scraped against the side of a poda-poda and come to a standstill. Verbal abuse was shouted. Passengers from the poda-poda joined the palaver. And the truck drivers pitched in for all they were worth. An unremarkable incident, except that the most vociferous participant in this slanging-match was, I observed, a young man standing on the tailgate of the truck and wearing the ubiquitous Forgive and Reconcile for National Development T-shirt.

In this chapter I explore the lived reality behind the rhetoric of reconciliation, and examine the relation of notions of truth and justice to power. I am particularly interested in the contrast between what Veena Das calls 'cosmologies of the powerful' and 'cosmologies of the powerless' (1995:139–140) – the ways in which explanations of violence, as well as strategies for enduring it, reflect people's differential command of social power. My point of departure is the war experience of a young Kuranko woman. Though I heard and recorded many stories in the course of my few weeks' fieldwork in Sierra Leone, Fina Kamara's story is not untypical. And though I present it here as a single case, I think it illuminates something of what is at stake for most Sierra Leoneans in the postwar period, and why, in the words of one refugee, 'The government declares that the war is over, but for us it still goes on'.

Fina Kamara's Story

The day I went to see Fina Kamara in the amputee camp at Murray Town, the question uppermost in my mind had less to do with the trauma of war than how a person addresses the losses she has suffered, the injustices he has endured. How, when lives are shattered, can life be renewed?

Exactly three years before I had read a story in the *Guardian Weekly* under the headline 'Machete Terror Stalks Sierra Leone'. It concerned a rebel attack on the Kuranko village of Kondembaia in

April 1998, and its focus was the ordeal of a young Kuranko woman and her six year-old daughter.

Fina Kamara's husband was my field assistant's maternal uncle, and so we had little difficulty in locating her. After parking the Toyota 4-Runner and asking some kids if he knew where the people from Kondembaia were living, Sewa led the way through a labyrinth of alleys to the centre of the camp. Though many of the refugees were living in makeshift dwellings, made of white- and blue-striped UN plastic tarps pulled over lashed poles, Fina occupied a room in a disused barracks.

I recognised her at once from the photo that had appeared in the *Guardian*, and after Sewa had introduced me, I told Fina of the fieldwork I used to do in Kondembaia, and the recordings I had made of Keti Ferenke's stories. I then showed her the clipping from the *Guardian* that I had bought with me. She looked at it without emotion or interest before passing it on to the other refugees who, out of curiosity, had now joined us. No one commented.

I asked Fina if she would mind if I tape-recorded her story. She raised no objection, but wanted to know if she should speak in Krio or Kuranko. I suggested she speak in Kuranko.

We were hiding in the bush for three months, she began. We were afraid the RUF[1] might come at any time and attack the town. But then we received messages from Freetown and from ECOMOG[2] to come out of the bush and return to town. So we came out of the bush.

One day we went to our farm to plant groundnuts. We returned to town that afternoon. Suddenly, we heard gunshots. Because there were ECOMOG soldiers in Kondembaia, we were used to hearing gunfire, but this time we were confused.

The RUF came suddenly. They shot many people. They stacked the bodies under the cotton tree. Then they grabbed us. Their leader said they were going to kill us too. But then they sent their boys to bring a knife. My daughter Damba was six. They took her from me and cut off her hand. After that they cut off all our hands. One man died because of the bleeding. We ran. We fell to the ground. After some time we got up. Damba said, Mummy, I am thirsty. By now all the houses were on fire. We went behind one of the houses. One of the RUF boys came and said, What are you doing there? I said, I want to give water to my daughter. I gave Damba some water. Then I sat down and tied her on my back. We began running again, but they stopped us in the backyard of one of the houses. One RUF girl said, You move one step and I will shoot you. I had to go back. But there was a place behind the houses. We went down there. After a while I felt hungry. I found a mango but could not eat it because my blood was all over it. A little while later I overheard the RUF saying that it was time for them to leave. When they had gone, I found my son, and tied Damba on my back again and went to the bush. From there I came out on the road and sat down. I met my husband and uncle there. Everyone was crying. I told them to stop crying. We went to our farm, and in the morning we set off for Kabala. We did not reach Kabala that day because of the pain. It took us two days. People in Kabala said we were lucky; the Red Cross was there. After treating us they brought us by helicopter to Freetown here. We were taken to Connaught Hospital. They treated us there. Then we were taken to Waterloo. When the RUF invaded Freetown, we had to flee from Waterloo. We fled to the Stadium. From there we were brought to this camp here. If you ask me, this is all I know. We were ordinary people, we were farmers, we had nothing to do with the government. Whenever I think about this, and about the time they cut off my hand, and my daughter's hand, only six years of age, I feel so bad. Our children are here now. They are not going to school. Every morning we are given bulgar. Not enough for us. We are really suffering here. We only hope this war will come to an end and that we will be taken back to our own places. If we go back home, we have our own people there who will help us.

Though I asked Fina some questions, I was oppressed by my inability to respond to her story with anything other than sympathetic words. Even giving her what money I had felt like an empty gesture. And as I retraced my steps to the vehicle with Sewa, down the fetid alleyways, past other amputees, I felt like a thief, or voyeur.

As we drove back toward the city, across the bridge, I saw that the tide was in. It made me think how, in the ordinary course of events, change occurs gradually, almost imperceptibly, allowing us time to adjust, to acclimatise, even to ignore it. So we age. Things wear out, and decay. The tide ebbs or flows. But when an accident happens, our whole world is changed utterly in a split second. We have no time to think. No time to prepare. Suddenly, we are sundered from our lives, from all that we have been, and plunged into nothingness. The shock is absolute.

Three and a half years had passed since Fina Kamara's world fell apart, and she was still struggling to grasp how this could have happened. The rebels came and went within an hour. In this short time they murdered fifty people and mutilated another ten or fifteen. They also set fire to every building in Kondembaia, save the mosque which they used as a kitchen, and the school, the church, and a house where they stashed their belongings. Though Fina had spoken of the RUF, many of the rebels were in fact young junta soldiers, avenging their ouster from power a few weeks earlier when the Nigerian-led ECOMOG reinstated the elected government of Ahmad Tejan Kabbah. Unable to defeat the ECOMOG soldiers or the Civil Defense militias, they took their revenge on the defenceless people who had allegedly voted for the government, or sheltered and supported the CDF. Of all this, Fina Kamara knew nothing. We are ordinary people, she had told me. All we do is go to our farms.

I had asked her, Do you think you will ever learn to live with what has happened?

I will never forget.

Would it make any difference to you, if the people that did these dreadful things were punished?

I no longer waste my anger on them. But I will never forget what they did. When they burned my house, how can I forget that? When I look at my hand, how can I ever forget? I feel the pain constantly. Even now, talking to you, I feel it. At times, I can feel my fingers, even though they are not there.

When I saw my old friend Noah[3] the following day, I told him of my visit to the amputee camp, and of Fina Kamara's description of the phantom pain she felt in her hand. The embodied memory of all she had suffered. But I was perplexed, I told Noah, by the way that Fina had explained her feelings toward those who had visited this suffering upon her, and upon her village.

Noah was ready for this conversation. He had come to see me at his brother's house the day before, only to be turned away at the gate. The soldiers and security guards had refused him entry, though they knew he was S.B's brother.[4] Even now, the humiliation and insult rankled. You see, he said, how I am shut out. How I have no one inside who can help me. How I have to look outside for help.

I am sorry.

It is not your fault.

I told Noah that when I had asked Fina Kamara what she might do to redress the damage that had been done to her and her daughter she said, There is nothing I can do. And when I asked her what she thought about reconciliation, she used the phrase *m'bara hake*[5] *to an ye*, which Sewa translated as 'I can forgive, but I cannot forget.' What exactly did she meant by this?

It's what you might say, Noah said, when someone offends or hurts you, and you are powerless to retaliate. If, for instance, someone takes something from you without justification. Or insults and humiliates you for no good reason. Say a hawk came out of the blue and seized one of your chickens. What can you do? You can't get it back. The hawk has flown away. You have no means of hunting it down, or killing it. All you can do is accept, and go on with your life. But you don't really forgive, you don't really forget. You simply accept that there's nothing you can do to change what has happened. Look at me. I have no way of taking my revenge on the rebels who took away my livelihood, but at least I can rid myself of them. I can shut them out of my mind. I can expel them from my life.[6]

Noah's words reminded me of a passage in Hannah Arendt's *The Human Condition* (1958:237*)*. Forgiveness implies neither loving those that hate you, nor absolving them from their crime, nor even understanding them ('they know not what they do'); rather, it is a form of redemption, in which one reclaims one's own life, tearing it free from the oppressor's grasp, and releasing oneself from those thoughts of revenge and those memories of one's loss that might otherwise keep one in thrall to one's persecutor forever.

If I say *i hake a to nye*, Noah continued, I am freeing myself of the effects of your hatred. I am refusing to hate back. But this doesn't mean that justice will not be done. Most of us here feel that God sees everything, and that God will mete out punishment in His own good time. That's why we say, *Alatala si n'hake bo a ro*, God will take out my anger on him. So I might say, *m'bara n'te to Al'ma*, I have left it up to God. Same as they say in Krio, I don lef mi yon to God. I think this is what Fina Kamara meant. She was not saying that she forgives the RUF, but that she is leaving it up to God to see that justice is done. Because how can you ever be reconciled to someone who has killed your father or cut off your hand? Reconciliation, forgiveness, forgetting ... these are all relative terms. In Sierra Leone right now, we are letting sleeping dogs lie. You understand? We are fed up with the war. Fed up with atrocities. If we talk about the war, it is not because we are plotting revenge or want to prolong the suffering. We simply do not want it to happen again.

Writing up my notes that evening at the Cape Sierra hotel, I kept being drawn back to this issue of reconciliation and revenge. Though Fina Kamara and Noah had found it expedient to give up all thought of payback, this did not mean they they rejected the possibility of retaliation or the principle of lex talionis. Indeed payback is an open and vexed question in Sierra Leone. For who will see that justice is done? How can apologies atone for the material and social losses people have suffered. Who will pay for reparations? And will the trial of war criminals in Special Courts set up at both national and village levels simply rub salt into old wounds, arouse bitter memories, cause resentment and enmity, and set in train another cycle of violence (Jackson 2002:57, 62, 164–167). The people I spoke to were realists, acutely aware of what they could and could not do. If S.B. Marah was less forgiving when he spoke of the RUF, it was not because his anger was stronger but because he was in a stronger position, as a senior politician, to see that justice was done. His attitude to his thirteen-month long detention in 1974, was, however, very different. When I asked him what he felt as he recounted his experiences in Pademba road, and the judicial murder of his peers, he said, It is painful, but it has happened, it has happened. It was politics. It was the kind of thing you had to expect. But the RUF atrocities were something else. Something beyond the pale, something outside the bounds of what was human, and could not be forgiven. Though S.B., Fina Kamara, and Noah were as different as any human beings could be, I had been struck by their sober sense of what, in any given situation, was possible and what was impossible – of where the limits of their freedom lay. All too often in the West, ideas like truth and freedom are discussed in total abstraction. We are encouraged in the belief that there is nothing we cannot do if we put our minds to it. That there is no corner of the universe that is intrinsically beyond our understanding and control. No limit to our power to manipulate genes, to prolong life, to alleviate suffering, and to find personal fulfilment.

But what struck me so forcibly about Fina Kamara's story was not only her awareness of her own powerlessness, but the absence of any dwelling on the self. There are, I think, two reasons why this was so. First, is the Kuranko habit of recounting one's experience, not as a singular biography but as a series of shared critical events (Jackson 1989:20). Thus, Fina and others who suffered in the war were well aware that the violence was arbitrary. If they were victims, it was because the rebels classified everyone who was not for them as being against them, and because they simply happened to be in the wrong place at the wrong time. It was not that they were singled out on account of their specific identity. This is vividly conveyed in the way Fina relates her story. It is only at the moment when her arm is severed, or when she tries to eat the bloody mango, that her narrative consciousness is fully on herself. At other times she is a part of the village, one among many, and she recounts events as they happened to 'us.'[7] As a corollory of this emphasis on 'we' rather than 'I', Kuranko tend to construct experience as intersubjective rather than intrapsychic, though from an empirical point of view each obviously entails the other. Alhough people suffered humiliation, bereavement, mutilation and grievous loss in the war no one spoke of unhinged minds, of broken spirits, or of troubled souls. And healing was sought, not through words, but deeds. Not through therapy but through things. Fees to send children to school. Cement and roofing iron to rebuild houses. Grain. Micro-credit.

Food. Medicines. It may well be that a diagnostic label like Post Traumatic Stress Disorder is empirically justified,[8] but it is imperative that we acknowledge that intrapsychic wounds are not the burning issue for Sierra Leoneans, but rather the material means that are needed to sustain life, and ensure a future for one's children.[9]

There was a full moon, and I lay on my bed for some time, gazing out the window into the milky blueness of the tropical night, and imagining that I could hear, beyond the noise of the hotel generator, the sound of the sea pounding its fists on the beach. Perhaps it was because I was missing my own children that my thoughts turned to Fina Kamara, and the question as to when she would see her daughter again. An aid agency (she did not know which one) had taken Damba to the US for advanced medical treatment, leaving Fina with no way of communicating with her, and no idea when Damba would return to Freetown. I had no way of knowing how this unidentified agency had justified such a prolonged separation of mother and daughter. Perhaps the overriding consideration had been rescuing Damba from the brutality of war, and giving her a prosthetic limb, rather than the bond between her and her mother. In her despair, Fina had no option but to look for God. Yet, I asked myself, have we in our complacency arrogated the power of God to ourselves, and as a consequence placed people like Fina in the invidious position of having to look to us for what we may not, in reality, have the means to give.

Notes

1   Revolutionary United Front, otherwise known as the rebels.

2   Economic Community of West African States Monitoring Group – a military force, made up mainly of Nigerian troops, that was brought into Sierra Leone to quell the rebellion.

3   Noah B. Marah worked with me as a research assistant during my initial fieldwork among the Kuranko in northern Sierra Leone (1969–70, 1972, 1979).

4   Noah's brother, S.B. Marah, was a prominent Sierra Leonean politician, and Leader of the House in Ahmad Tejan Kabbah's SLPP government. I was researching his lifestory.

5   Hake is sometimes translated as 'sin', though the word covers a multitude of motives – hatred, ill-will, malice, envy – and distracts from the principle of

retributive justice that lies behind it. In Kuranko thought, intersubjective relationships are governed by reciprocity, so that if a person offends, wrongs, or injures
another person without justification, the offence calls for payback (tasare). This
compensatory action may be effected through several means. It may follow a
court hearing, in which case the offender must indemnify the person to whom
injury has been caused. It may follow a verbal apology, in which the offender
begs forgiveness. It may, if recourse to legal means or the workings of individual
conscience are unavailing, lead the injured party to take matters into his own
hand and seek sorcery as a form of revenge. Alternatively, if the injured party
feels that no worldy agency can secure redress, he may be inclined to leave mat-
trers in the hands of God. In a previous discussion of hake (Jackson 1982:29–30)
I speak of automatic redress, in which an unprovoked and unjustified offence
will boomerang back against the offender, particularly if the would-be victim
is protected by magical medicines. In conversations with Kuranko informants
in January–February 2002, however, such redress was thought to require divine
agency. As Noah put it, 'People feel that God is just and omnipotent. One way
or another He'll avenge the crime or wrong-doing.'

6   Four years before, Noah had been living in Lunsar, where he underwent an
operation for glaucoma. But the rebels were threatening Lunsar at the time, and
the two expatriot doctors had to flee the town within a day of performing the
second operation on Noah's eyes. They had given me medication, Noah said,
and bandaged my eyes, but when the rebels broke into my house and took me
captive I had to leave everything behind. They taunted me. They said 'Pappy,
here, drink' and thrust a bottle of beer at me. I said I didn't drink. They pushed
a cannabis cigarette into my mouth. I told them I didn't smoke. I said: 'Would I
eat if I were not hungry?' From Lunsar we walked to Masimera where we stopped
for two days. I asked if I could talk to their C.O. They said 'What! A civilian
like you wanting to see our C.O.!' One of them lifted his weapon to show what
would happen if I went on pushing my luck. Four days later, Noah said, the
rebels abandoned him in a Temne village. His eyes were no longer bandaged,
and he was in a lot of pain. In the months that followed he lost the sight of one
eye, and now had only limited vision in the other. Unable to return to school
teaching - which he was doing when I first met him - and with little hope of
finding other work, he survived in Freetown on his wits, scrounging money to
buy rice and food for his family and school fees for his kids.

7   That all villagers were equal in the eyes of the rebels, may ironically have helped
them bear the trauma they experienced, for though RUF violence destroyed
the lives of so many, it has reinforced a sense of solidarity among the survivors.
This solidarity was clearly evident when the Civilian Defence Force war widows,
orphans, and ex-combatants Association was launched in Kabala, northern Sierra Leone, on January 11 2002 with the aim of rebuilding villagers, clinics, and
schools, of offering vocational training in gara-dying, carpentry, and tailoring,
and providing medicines and micro-credit to villagers.

8   Allan Young argues that PTSD is 'not timeless, nor does it possess an intrinsic
unity. Rather, it is glued together by the practices, technologies, and narratives

with which it is diagnosed, studied, treated, and represented, and by the various interests, institutions, and moral arguments that mobilized these efforts and resources' (1995:5). Though historically and socially constructed, this does not mean, however, that what we label trauma or PTSD does not signify profoundly real experiences of human distress (ibid:5–6).

9   These opposing view of reconciliation were ever-present in the Truth and Reconciliation Commission hearings in South Africa. While Archbishop Desmond Tutu, for example, saw reconciliation idealistically, in Christian terms, as a matter of saving one's soul and forgiving one's enemies ('You can only be human in a humane society. If you live with hatred and revenge in your heart, you dehumanize not only yourself, but your community'), Vice-President Thabo Mbeki placed far less emphasis on individual redemption, stressing instead the creation of a new and viable society (Krog 1999:110–111). The same difference in emphasis emerged from debates over the allegedly self-indulgently 'self-centred' attitude of whites (concerned solely with personal amnesty and absolution) and the so-called 'we-centredness' of blacks (concerned more with healing a damaged nation through piacular rituals, and new forms of social solidarity and shared belief (Krog op.cit:160–161).

References

Arendt, Hannah 1958: *The Human Condition*. Chicago: University of Chicago Press.

Das, Veena 1995: *Critical Events: an Anthropological Perspective in Contemporary India*. Delhi: Oxford University Press.

Jackson, Michael 1982: *Allegories of the Wilderness: Ethics and Ambiguity in Kuranko Narratives*. Bloomington: Indiana University Press.

Jackson, Michael 1989: *Paths Toward a Clearing: Radical Empiricism and Ethnographic Inquiry*. Bloomington: Indiana University Press.

Jackson, Michael 2002: *The Politics of Storytelling: Violence, Transgression, and Intersubjectivity* Copenhagen: Museum Tusculanum Press.

Krog, Antjie 1999: *Country of my Skull*. London: Jonathan Cape.

Sebald, W.G. 2001: *Austerlitz*. London: Penguin.

Young, Allan 1995: *The Harmony of Illusions: Inventing Post-Traumatic Stress Disorder*. Princeton, New Jersey: Princeton University Press.

FRANCINE LORIMER

Stories of Strangers Around the Fire

In this paper, I will visit a Sankt Hans festival that took place on June 23, 2001, in Copenhagen, Denmark, and revisit the site of my fieldwork in Cape York, Australia, in order to explore attitudes to outsiders in two very different cultures, and to make a case for a particular way of telling a story as a strategy for ethnographic understanding.[1]

Let me begin with a Danish popular song that is sung on Sankt Hans Eve,

> We love our land
> When the blessed Christmas lights the star
> in the tree with a sparkle in every eye,
> When in the spring every bird over the fields
> and at the shore lets their voice
> form into trills of praise
> We celebrate your rule over country land and city street
> When your harvest is in the barn, Sankte Hans,
> that is made of summer's heart so warm, so glad,
> but the most beautiful garland
> is yours, Sankte Hans!
> That is made of summer's heart so warm, so glad.
>
> We love our land
> But midsummer most –
> when every cloud over the field sends blessings,
> when there are masses of flowers,
> and when the cattle are yoked –

gives the most abundant gift to the diligent hands.
When we do not plough and harrow and flatten the earth,
when the cow her midday meal grazes in the clover
then go the young ones to dance
on your bid, Sankte Hans!
Like the foal and the lamb,
that frolic in the pastures.

We love our land,
and with the sword in hand,
it will be clear to outside forces that we are prepared.
But against the spirit of unpeace
over field, at the shore,
we will light the fire on our forefathers' gravemounds.
Every town has its witches, and every parish its trolls,
we will keep them from our lives with fires of joy.
We want peace in this land,
Sankte Hans, Sankte Hans!
It can be won, when the hearts never grow cold with doubt![2]

Sankt Hans Eve comes at the end of the school year, and always on June 23 – one or two days after the summer solstice. In Denmark, this night is celebrated by burning a bonfire, on which there is sometimes placed the effigy of a witch. While the fire burns, people sing a number of popular, 'traditional' Sankt Hans Eve songs. It is better when there is a witch on the bonfire, a Danish friend told me, and it is better if the song is sung while the witch is burning. Sankt Hans Eve is an event that both children and parents attend; they might meet up with friends in a neighbour's back yard, gather by a fire on the beach if they live near the coast or, if they live in the city – as in my case – they may go along to Fælledparken, the large park that straddles Nørrebro and Østerbro. Fælledparken might be translated as 'the commons'. There are football fields marked out on the grassy expanse. People gather in this park to celebrate May 1st, as well as other events throughout the year. While the bonfire that is lit there on this night is huge, the evening is not a major event in the Danish calendar. But it is a warm event, as the song says. Being close to the solstice, it stays light until late at night, and it is a time to celebrate summer with friends.

When I picked up my children from school earlier that day, I was not even aware that it was Sankt Hans Eve. But while I stood waiting for my children, a Danish friend, Helene, invited us to join a group of her friends and their children who were meeting at Fælledparken that evening.

Four hours later, my children and I arrived at this city park to find several hundred people already there. It was immediately clear that we were entering a scene of play. There were many families and friends lying on blankets, playing outdoor party games. And the play was open. It was among little groups, but it spilled out and touched neighbours. As my son dribbled his ball through the crowd, one young man after another stole it from him and gave it some deft kicks before returning it with a chuckle.

We met up with Helene and her friends, and Helene told me the story of Sankt Hans Eve. She said, 'All the witch effigies, once they were burnt, were believed to fly to a place in Germany where they gathered.'[3] 'But in the old days', her friend added, 'they burnt real witches'. 'Yes', said Helene, 'beautiful women who attracted a lot of men.'

One of the children joined in the conversation. He had received a negative school report. A woman added that her daughter also had had difficulties with her teacher. I had the impression that it was a release for them to let go of these failures, to lay them out on the grass with the food and wine.

Meanwhile, Freya, my 6 year-old daughter and her classmate, in pink and white, wandered around the crowd looking for feathers. They were totally absorbed in what they were doing, and wandered out of sight until they got lost and then picked their way through the crowd back to us.

At almost ten in the evening, I decided to move up to the fire with the children to look at the witch mannequin and to see when the fire was going to be lit. We squirmed to the front of the crowd and could see that there were patches of flame licking the wood. We sat down and gazed, and very soon the huge pile of wood was ablaze. A man with a rake warned us that the whole pile might collapse or the flame might expand, so the crowd retreated, inching back as the fire grew. The children were mesmerized. One said: 'It's beautiful'. I noticed couples embracing, holding hands, gazing into each others' eyes, and I wondered what this event meant to the adults here.

'Summer!', shot back a friend when I later shared my musings with her. She told me that Sankt Hans Eve is a time in Denmark when summer is played out, contrasted – as in the song – with the cold and confinement of winter time. Winter is a time for sharing a meal with family or friends around a candle flame to light up the long hours of darkness (Ardener 1992). In spring, people take walks through fields and forests to enjoy the shimmering of the young beech leaves (Damsholt 2000) and in autumn, to pick mushrooms – perhaps with members of a mushrooming society. These small ritual happenings are a way of celebrating the seasonal landscape 'together with-'.

However, when the fire at Fælledparken began to rage, it was the children who told me what they felt, and they spoke what they imagined so vividly that the boundary between play and reality seemed to become blurred. Although Joshua, my ten-year-old son, later remarked that he was just 'imagining out loud', it seemed that the younger children needed me to mark the difference.

When the flames reached the adult-sized witch at the top of the pyre, she caught alight, and what appeared to be a skeleton head bent forward and toppled into the flames below. Mette, my daughter's classmate, grew scared and shrank back. 'Is the witch still here?' she asked me. 'Where is it?'

I told her that it wasn't really a witch. It was just some stuffed clothes. But she replied, 'I want to go back to my Mum.' For a few moments there was chaos. The other children seemed to be drawn closer to the flames, completely entranced, and beyond my influence. Mette was full of fear and shrinking back. I called to the other children to leave but they were defiant. They were not moving. I could go, they were staying. So I told them to sit together, holding hands, and I quickly brought Mette back to my friends' picnic. By this time, however, Mette wanted to return to the fire.

When we returned, we found the other children sitting down calmly, in front of the crowd. One girl had her head in another's lap, protecting her face from the intensity of the glare. We sat down and watched. My son exclaimed in wonder, 'The witch is coming out in the smoke. And all the women who breathe in the smoke are going to become witches.' Then he turned to me and exclaimed, 'Don't breathe in the smoke!' (Later that night, as we headed home, Joshua pointed to the heavy clouds in the sky and commented, 'There's a thousand witches up there, just waiting to come down to earth.')

'If I saw a witch, I would *beat it up!*' Freya exclaimed, as she gazed at the fire, and she dramatized meeting a witch, baring her teeth and clenching her fists.

Mette again turned to me: 'Is the witch cross?' I replied, 'Of course she is! Wouldn't *you* be cross if a crowd of people burned *you*?' She responded: 'Yes.' But then she said, 'But how *can* she be cross? She's not real!' I responded: 'No. She's not real. But if she *was* real, she would be cross, don't you think?' 'Yes.'

Joshua repeated, 'The witch is coming out of the fire; you see all those sparks: those are her eyes.'

The witch had been burnt, the fire had stabilized, and the mood of the crowd was changing. People were relaxing, soaking up the event, and some African men were drumming and dancing. A few adult couples ran around the fire, close to the flames. A young man with dark skin whom I was sitting next to turned to me and asked with an accent where I was from. I said, 'Australia.' He asked, 'What language do they speak in Australia?' and I replied, 'English – or an Aboriginal language.' I then asked him, 'Where are you from?' He replied: 'I'm from Denmark.' I said 'Oh.' He added, 'But originally I was from Afganistan.' I asked, 'Were you born in Denmark?' 'No. I was born in Afganistan. I came to Denmark four years ago.' We were warming up for a conversation about how we each found being in Denmark when his friends signalled to him that they were leaving, and he left with a smile. After he had gone, one of the children turned to me and said: 'Don't talk to that black man.'

I was shocked by this child's idea that I should not speak to another person in the crowd because he was 'black'. My mind began to wander as a way of making sense of this childish imagination. And

I wondered whether the child had picked up on the theme of black from the conversation we had been having before the bonfire.

As we had picnicked together, my adult friends had told us about other festivals in Denmark. One man told us, 'In the old days, they used to put black cats in a barrel for the whole winter, feeding it in the barrel, until, at the carnival of Fastelavn, they would beat the barrel. If the cat survived, it was set free, but it often died of shock'[4]. But, while the theme of black seemed to remain, the conversation drifted away from the subject of cats. Another man had commented that the neighbourhood in which we had recently bought a house – Nørrebro – was no longer safe to be in at night because of its high immigrant population. By contrast, in Johannesburg, 'blacks' lived in separate parts of town. This man had lived in both Johannesburg and Copenhagen, and of the two cities, he found Johannesburg the safer. 'The only thing about Johannesburg is that you need to know which parts to avoid.'

In fact, the subject of the presence of immigrants in Denmark pervaded the media, and lurked in the back of many conversations I had with Danish friends. Denmark was at the time involved in a very public debate on how to treat its small but conspicuous population of immigrants, asylum seekers and refugees. The reactionary Dansk Folkeparti would later win enough votes for its anti-immigration platform to influence government policy. Some of my friends' remarks seemed to reflect the expectation that their lives were lived in terms of a clearcut ordering of society into people with whom one belonged and people with whom one did not belong.

The day before, a Danish friend had given me some advice about my plans to enrol the children in a sports club as a way of learning some Danish and feeling part of the place. She told me that it would be futile to have my children go to a sports club here because children go to sports clubs *with* their friends, not to *meet* friends. I said, 'But I had hoped that at least my children might meet some other children in the neighbourhood.' She replied: 'But I wouldn't let *my* children play with just anyone in my neighbourhood! This is a city, just like any other city.' Earlier, this friend had described our suburb as the most 'interesting' place to live. Interesting from a distance. The witch effigy is interesting, too. Drawing people together in front of a fire – to watch it burn.[5]

By about 10:30, the attention at Fælledparken was less on the fire, and people began to dance to the drums, or hug and kiss. My picnicking friend said: 'It's pagan!' and laughed.[6] The witch had been burnt. It was not real, it was many years in the past, a *long* time ago, as Mette had earlier stressed. But as I listened and watched both the adults and the children during this evening, I was intrigued by the same question that Kristi Hjemdahl ponders when describing Scandinavian amusement parks (Hjemdahl, article in this volume): Was this witch-burning event a remembering or an engendering? And, as Hjemdahl also observes, I realized that it was through the children's eyes that I experienced the event as something that was not an imitation of an archaic past, an icon of tradition; it was happening very much now, and in relation to us. The dark forces of witch and troll had been cast over to Germany, leaving only the positive power of our belonging. But as the witch was burnt, for these children, she was released into the present: her eyes were the sparks; the smoke was her anger. 'Is she angry (at us)?' Mette wanted to know. It was fun to play with the idea, as my son had done, that, as soon as it had been burnt, the witch's dark spirit did not fly away as it was supposed to, but gathered in the smoke or in the clouds, ready to redescend on the people of Denmark. 'Don't breath in the smoke!'

Can we make some connection between the vividness of these children's imaginations and the talk about immigrants that I was hearing among the adults? Is there any connection between the fantastic dark forces of witches and trolls, and the presence of foreigners in Denmark today? The witches had been cast out, but the beat that people began dancing to was being played by African men. I could not help wondering what my companion who had lived in Johannesburg thought about this. Were his comments that immigrants were a hazard to public safety a way of magically putting them, like the witch, back out onto the other side of the Danish border?

It was past 11 o'clock when Sankt Hans Eve came to an end. I walked with my own two children to Trianglen at Østerbro to wait for a bus. As we waited, we were passed by a truck festooned with Danish flags, full of graduating high school students. They waved and cheered, and two young men displayed their bare bottoms. The children watched, incredulous. 'That's not real!' Freya commented. 'Yes it is', I laughed. Joshua asked, 'Why are they doing that?' I told them, 'Because they are celebrating finishing school. Everything's upside down tonight. Students are showing their bottoms, we're up at midnight!' Freya asked me, 'Why are they waving to us?' I said, 'Because they want to share their happiness with the whole world. So they go to each other's houses, and on the way, they wave to everyone they see, and everyone feels happy for them.'

The bus took us to Svanemøllen station, and from there we caught the last train home. It was very late, and the children seemed to be enveloped in their own imaginative worlds, in a kind of revery, as we walked the last stretch to our apartment. They sang softly to themselves about their friends, the people they loved, and how they could triumph over their particular problems. It struck me that something had been released at least in my children, as they walked home after the latest night out they had ever had; they had played, and something had been played out. They were not alone. They had been mesmerized by the fire and the witch falling into it; they had been amazed by the students' festive play. Descriptions have been written of the act of displaying one's naked bottom as an act of hostility. But to my mind, this act seemed to be at this moment an act of extreme belonging. That which was the most private about them, in this carnivalesque atmosphere, became a symbol of their commonality.[7] A Kuku-Yalanji Aboriginal man once described to me how prepubescent girls used to undergo initiation. At one point, an old man would bare his behind in front of them. The girls' courage was tested if their faces showed no emotion. In both these events, baring bottoms took place between people who shared some form of intimacy. The children felt all this, and by the end of the evening, they sang about the world that they felt a *part* of. Play had made strangers into family. But in the course of this play, the opposite had also taken place: a casting out of 'otherness', in the form of the dark force of the witch. 'Every town has its witches and its trolls', goes the song. The ironic twist is that a new version of the 'Other' – the ethnic other – was in the crowd now, and the people I spoke with, through their talk, seemed to be quite unconsciously acting out this very old practice of keeping this very new kind of Other out. I wondered whether, had my son been obviously foreign, the young men in the crowd at the beginning of the evening would have stolen his ball, kicked it around and then returned it with a chuckle.

I have tried here to describe how, on the innocent Danish festivity of Sankt Hans Eve, certain details conveyed the tension that Danes are caught up in at this moment of history between, on the one hand, a desire to reach out towards immigrants in Denmark, and, on the other, a deep-seated sentiment that Danish citizenship is connected to the celebration of rituals that bind people with their land and its old traditions.

Let me now turn to a description of a story told to me by Steve, the husband of Sue, who is an elder of a Kuku-Yalanji extended family that I lived with in Cape York, Australia during 1993–4, and revisited in 1995 and 1999. Steve's story is relevant here because it is also about strangers. Steve is not Kuku-Yalanji. He is Lama Lama, and the account sees him driving back to his wife's country after having been to a land claim meeting in Laura, near his traditional country. As with Denmark today, Cape York has experienced sweeping demographic changes. The difference is that in Cape York, the changes have happened for over a hundred and twenty years, and whole Aboriginal populations have been radically diminished or removed to other locations as a result. Such was the case for Steve's people.

Despite this, there continues to exist a strong tradition of belonging to country through an intricate and robust community of social connections through kinship and marriage. Sue and Steve live within this web of belonging, which is very much connected to the land that Sue, as a Kuku-Yalanji, has grown up in and has a clan-based affiliation to. But Sue's country lies on the coastline of one of the most popular tourist locations in the world, near Cape Tribulation, and many strangers pass through the place, or live there for a short time. Kuku-Yalanji avoid these people, almost as if they did not exist. They live their own lives, in relation to their own people and their neighbours, and let the strangers come and go. This is more difficult, however, on the shared space of the public highway, where Aboriginal people risk encountering strangers outside the safety of their own place. On one occasion, when I was on the same stretch of road that appears in Steve's story, a vehicle tooted its horn. This is a gesture of greeting in the outback, but we were unsure of the meaning of this particular toot, so we slowed down, turned around, and prepared to have a conversation with the driver. Immediately, Sue and her sisters in the back dropped to the floor, and remained there while we made contact with the driver. When we drove off again, I asked them why they had done this.

'Strangers', replied Sue's sister. 'We don't like strangers'.

So Steve's story is about strangers – a theme that ignites a certain dread in Kuku-Yalanji people's hearts. I tell it here because of how and why Steve told me the story. I decided later that Steve *chose* to tell me this story because he wanted me to see strangers in the same way that *he* saw them. But he does not say this directly. Rather, the power of Steve's story is in its dramatic details, in the meaning that is alluded to them, and in the time that it takes to tell the story – and to draw the listener into the moment of its happening. Here is a story, then, that somewhat echoes my account of Sankt Hans Eve. I was also seeking to draw an audience into seeing something (in my case it was not a category of person so much as an event) in the same way I saw it. I will share Steve's story, and then reflect on the extent to which both storytelling and contemporary anthropology work to make claims for the truth value of seeing something in a certain way, though aware that their audiences may very likely choose to see it differently.

I had lived with Steve and Sue for nearly a year. At this point, I was on my own with my two-year old son, and was planning to drive alone with him on the three-hour trip down to Cairns. Neither Steve nor Sue made any reference to this plan of mine until the evening before I was due to leave, when the three of us happened to be sitting together by their campfire. Steve remarked, 'You know, Francine, Sue and I were just thinking about this lady who got kidnapped. It was last year, eh?' He turned to Sue, who repeated,

'Last year.' Steve went on, 'She went all the way from Mossman to the Palmer River. Well, she was a nurse, too. Well, these two men were on the road. One was fixing his car. I think he was just pretending. And they went onto the road and said: 'Hey! Stop! We got some problems here.' So she stopped and she said: 'You need any help?' She got out of the car. And then they told her, 'You're kidnapped!'

I said, 'Yeah?'

'That's right! And she was real scared. Well, they put her in the car, and drove off. They made her take out all her money, too. And there were police everywhere looking for her and those two men. And they got her car too.'

'Did they?'

'It was her friend's car. Anyway, they kept driving until it was dark, like about *this* time. Then when they got to the Palmer River, she opened the door and jumped out.'

'Really?'

'Yeah. And they was going fast too. She just opened the door when the car was driving real fast, and then jumped out. And she rolled over and over again. And she had cuts and scratches all over her. Well, when they realised she'd jumped out, they stopped the car. It was about from here to that tent before the car stopped. And then it reversed, 'cause they wanted to find her. But she ran into the bush, eh, and hid. It was real dark and they didn't have a torch, so after a while they got back in the car, and she listened for the car. They turned around and headed back down. Then, after a while, she heard a semi [large truck]. So she stood on the road and waved them down like this. [Steve put both hands in front of him and beckoned by bringing his hands down.] Well, semis have real good spotlights, eh, and they saw her from a long way away, waving like this [same action], standing on the road. They stopped and asked: 'what's wrong?' She said: 'I'm in trouble.' Sue and I were coming back from Laura festival and there were road-blocks everywhere, looking for those men. Well, the police said they might be walking. I think they must've driven the car over a cliff, ya know? And they found them a week later. Do you know where they found them?'

'No.'

'Western Australia.'

'That's pretty far.'

'That's right.' [PAUSE] So me and Sue a bit worried about you, ya know?

[PAUSE]

…driving by yourself…

[PAUSE]

…to Cairns.'

I laughed.

'Nah, well', said Steve, 'You gotta be careful, you know? About picking people up? Like there was this other time, these two ladies stopped. From Hope Vale. They saw a man – he was just lying down – they were *Bama* ladies[8] – and they stopped and said: 'You alright?' Well, he didn't say anything, ya know? He just looked in the car and saw there were just two ladies. Well, she rolled her window up and locked the door and they took off. And when they looked behind them, they saw his car taking off after them!'

'Really?'

'Yeah!' [laughing] But they had hi-lux, ya know?[9] And they just took off and left him behind! And one of the ladies had a baby, too, like Josh. Well, she was just hanging onto him! Oh yeah, and one of the men that kidnapped that nurse was half-Bama, you know?'

'Was he?'

'That's right. [PAUSE]. But he was nice. Yeah, he was real nice to her. The other guy was real mean.'

Among Aboriginal people in Australia, stories are told with skill and care. This reflects the importance of attending to the subject-matter that most stories are about, namely mythical ancestors and ritually important places. When the travels of mythical dreamtime figures are re-enacted in songs or stories, the exploits of these heroes are on another level descriptions of the sacred sites in the country. It is important for ritual reasons to get the details right. And people engage the help of an audience in this essential aspect of storytelling. 'This is my story', an Aboriginal man told me before beginning his account. 'You might have a different story'. And as the story is recounted, the audience affirms whether the details are indeed true, or whether the storyteller might have got it a little bit wrong. In some parts of Australia, this relationship between teller and listener draws on the principle that there is a relationship of reciprocity between people in different skin categories concerning rights and responsibilities towards ritual knowledge. According to this principle, the 'owners' of an area of land and its myths and rituals, rely on 'managers' (who stand in a different but related category of kinship) to guide them in all aspects of their ritual performance, supporting them and making sure they get it right. In this context, the telling of a story is thus at once a ritual and a social event: by the end, the story can indeed be affirmed to be 'true', and the social relationship between the performers and those who have participated in making the performance true is reconfirmed.[10] The story is straight, the path is right, the people are one.

During my fieldwork with Kuku-Yalanji people in Southeast Cape York, I found that even when people tell stories about mundane, everyday events, there is the same careful attention to getting the details of each place right. In these cases, too, I observed that what story is told, and how it is told, will depend on the relationship between the teller and the listeners. For a story to be told in the first place, there must be some prior social relationship. And, in the details of the telling, there is a great deal of attention to this relationship. This means that in the course of telling, there is a degree of uncertainty, a testing of the waters to see what kind of response the story receives, and people make small adjustments as the story goes along. And yet, as with the story that Steve told me of the hitch-hickers, stories delicately bring the listener around to the teller's way of seeing the world.

It is tricky to describe what other people might experience. George Devereux uses the case of the Hungarian Revolution to assert that it would be ridiculous to suggest that 'everyone who rebels and fights against an economically unfair and politically oppressive system has been *personally* underpaid and oppressed...' (1978:121). His point is that people who can be found acting together in a crowd towards a single purpose are each there for their own reasons, and it would therefore be false to assume that everyone felt exactly the same during the event. But certain details can strongly suggest a certain experiential reality. And by bringing the details of an event to an audience, one can encourage others to experience the same event in the way that the teller did. Steve did this by conveying through his story the experience of being kidnapped. He suggested to me the possibility that it might be dangerous to drive by myself; he encouraged me to suspend for a moment my own certainty that, as an adult, I was perfectly capable of driving alone on an outback road. But Steve did not tell me this message outright, probably because he did not think that I would heed him. As it was, when I finally registered the moral of the story, I laughed. Then the mood changed. Steve and Sue laughed too, and a second story was told, but this time with a suggestion of hilarity, as these two *Bama* women raced along the highway in their hi-lux, clinging onto a baby, being pursued by a crazy white stranger.

When he told his first story, Steve had my complete attention. I was that woman on the highway, in the bushes hiding from the two men, standing on the road, battered and bruised, waving my arms, *like this*. I was Sue and Steve being flagged down numerous times on the highway as they made their way southwards. Steve arranged the words of his story so that it became my story by describing the kidnapping in terms of the time and space that we were in. But when I knew the point of the story, I stopped it with a laugh – and then the next story was not about me. It was about these two *Bama* women, and it was funny. And it was more objective. And with this mood, Steve could introduce the fact that these two ominous kidnappers actually had some identity: one was a nice half-*Bama*, and the other was a 'real mean' white man. But these facts were not in the story as he first told it, whereas many other small details were, such as the fact that the woman was a nurse, and that she had borrowed her friend's car. Perhaps if Steve had mentioned why he was telling me the story beforehand, I would not have allowed myself to enter into the vividness of the details, and perhaps if Steve had told me that one of the kidnappers was Aboriginal and one was white, I might have framed the identity of the kidnappers in a way that allowed me to step out of the story. Steve fashioned his story in the way that he did because he did not want me to shut off the possibility that I, too, might feel fear – or at least a tinge of anxiety.

I also let 'telling details' speak – about the children's fear of the burning witch, their amazement at the carnivalesque graduation truck, and the preoccupations of some of the adults around me. In my 'story', too, there is an element of sculpting: it so happened that the witch on the pyre and the child's comment about not talking to black people occurred at the same place; but they were also juxtaposed in writing in order to invite reflection. My aim was to invite the audience to probe the emotions of fear and belonging that are triggered in times of social change. Ten years ago, Sankt Hans Eve might simply have been experienced as a celebration of summer. Burning the witch may have been described to me as a dramatic reenactment of a sinister time in history, and singing the songs might simply have evoked a feeling of togetherness. But with the changes that have swept through this old country, old activities take on new meanings. Why have some of my Danish friends said that they now feel uncomfortable singing songs, such as this one, that until recently they did not think twice about?

It is true that the way that an event is described – the way a photo is taken and cropped – itself constitutes the 'event', to a certain extent. So my depiction only suggests, in the same way that telling a story only suggests. But there is some value in allowing particular details of an event to be juxtaposed, and seeing what comes out of it. Whether in a description such as this, or a visual image or an adventure told by the fireside at night, highlighting 'telling details' through story-telling is one of the more creative ways we can respond to the inevitable tensions that come with new social moments. Perhaps *because* it takes a certain degree of artifice to frame the details in the right way.

What is the value of this complex task of drawing an audience into a crafted description? Storytelling has in the past been dismissed as simple or archaic, by contrast with other forms of narrative, which convey information or essay interpretations (Benjamin 1968). In a post-modern era, however, a form of discourse that is based on the assumption that the teller shares some elements of the same social context or history as the listener, and posits into the space between them certain details which invite response, make this genre a valuable tool for probing the complex questions of our current times.

In the days of E. Evans-Prichard, or even Margaret Mead, other peoples had other cultures, and these could be drawn upon reflectively in ways that allowed us to cast new light on our own culture (Asad 1973, Bhabha 1994). These days, we are aware that the very definition of the stranger or the other implies some hard looking at how we define ourselves. As Kristeva (1991) says, the stranger is within us as much as it is out there. This means that the focus is no longer about that macro division between self and other, such as that between insider and outsider, or good and evil; what is emerging is a much finer set of distinctions, between degrees of participation and forms of participation, and the different levels of social inclusion that these graded degrees and forms of participation bring into play (Baumann 1996).

Such accounts, in so far as they are 'true' to the detail of what took place, do not lie; but they also do not state: they invite participation first, then interpretation. This is one way of writing about new social situations in which there are new constellations of people; it is one way in which we can hold at the same moment the old thoughts that shape action almost without reflection, and new imaginings that have been barely articulated.

On the Sankt Hans Eve that I write about, it seemed to me that, for both the children and the adults, as well as the women and ethnic minorities in the crowd, it was possible to engage in the play of burning an effigy of a witch because it was a *symbolic* event. And the evil forces that the song and the witch reminded us of were the invisible evil of superstitious times, certainly not associated with the many foreigners at Fælledparken, who were sharing and delighting in the party. And yet, this non-real *playing* out of difference involved an uncanny parallelism with what I found to be a *real* defining of otherness in everyday life and a fear in the back of people's minds that the other would slip beyond definition. There is some satisfaction, then, in this 'old' practice of burning witches on the fire, and in this 'traditional' song that tells proudly of protecting this treasured and sacred Danish moment of the year/place in the world from the forces of unpeace, as the fires burn on the ancestral gravehills.

The spark that set me to writing this essay was my fascination with the contrasts and similarities between the preoccupations of the children and those of the adults. The children were anxious that the witch's power to subvert had not been curtailed by the burning. Her presence was frightening and very close. Her body was consumed by the fire, but her spirit could enter into the women who were watching her; she would come down in the rain again. These children's imaginations were quite different from the adult's experience of Sankt Hans Eve: where the children felt a living force that they could not control, the adults commemorated an ancient 'pagan' festival of fire, wine and dancing. And yet, the adults unwittingly mimicked the children's anxieties about the witch in their talk about immigrants. Parts of Copenhagen were described as unsafe because ethnic minorities lived in them. And here, too, there was an anxiety concerning the uncontrollable agency of the Other.

I found this comparison interesting because it occurred to me that the adults had forgotten the feelings of fear and vulnerability they might have had when witches were burned on the Sankt Hans Eves of their childhoods. And their talk about dangerous ethnic minorities was presented as though it was simply fact, or 'what people *say*', thereby precluding the observation that an element in the 'dangerousness' of recent immigrants in Denmark might be connected with Danish people's own fear of these immigrants' difference.

And yet, on a parallel with Aboriginal ritual accounts, the truth of my story depends on how my listeners receive it. While the details of a story have the power to evoke, there is a tremendous range in the possibilities of *what* is evoked. In this paper, I have given *my* story of a Sankt Hans Eve. As Steve would say, people who grew up in Denmark might have a different story. What Danes make of this account will involve their own way of experiencing Sankt Hans Eve, bringing up associations that could never be mine. And their experiences of the growing number of foreigners and second generation Danes will be more varied and nuanced than the anecdotes I have told here. But the details of my account sit there together and beg some kind of response. Perhaps the tension that I describe in the way that immigrants may both belong and not belong is parallel to the tension in the telling of a story between what the teller shares with an audience and that which separates the storyteller from the audience – and makes her want to tell the story.

As myself someone whom a Kuku-Yalanji would describe as 'European', but not Danish, I was perhaps sensitive to my experience of the feeling of belonging that pervaded this evening. This experience of belonging deeply touched both me and my children at the same time as it profiled elements of not-belonging. And I was struck by the contrast between the loudness of the 'pagan' witchburning and the graduation celebration, and the confident intimacy with which people spoke to me about immigrants as though their dangerousness was obvious. Was the witchburning really only about 'a *long* time ago'?

Story-telling implies some artifice. But perhaps the deliberate artifice of telling a story best captures my suspicion that emotions felt so keenly in childhood can find expression – without being recognized – in moments of adulthood. Which is why story-telling was the device I chose to convey my musings on how fear and play hovered around the edges of the rational during the various events I have described of that magic midsummer Sankt Hans Eve celebration.

Notes

1   I would like to thank Line Dalsgaard and Søren Christensen for help with the translation (although responsibility for the final translation is my own). I am also grateful to Line Dalsgaard, Sonja Marjasch, Lise Skov and Michael Jackson for their valuable comments on earlier drafts.

2   This song, which is also called 'Midsommervisen', was composed in 1885 by Holger Drachmann (1846–1908) and featured in the play 'Der var engang', which was performed in the Royal Theatre in 1887. Music for the song was composed by P.E. Lange-Muller. The song is now a feature of the festivities of Sankt Hans Eve, and there are many quotes of it, with accompanying music, on the internet. The Danish text which I have translated is as follows in its original version:

Vi elsker vort land,
når den signede jul
tænder stjernen i træet med glans i hvert øje,
når om våren hver fugl

over mark, under strand
lader stemmen
til hilsende triller sig bøje:
vi synger din lov over vej, over gade,
vi kranser dit navn når vor høst er i bir dog din, sankte Hans,
den er bunden af sommerens hjerter så varme, så glade,
men den skønneste krans
blir dog din, sankte Hans!
den er bunden af sommerens hjerter så varme, så glade.

Vi elsker vort land,
men ved midsommer mest,
når hver sky over marken velsignelsen sender,
når af blomster er flest,
og når kvæget i spand
giver rigeligst gave til flittige hænder;
når ikke vi pløjer og harver og tromler,
når koen sin middag i kløveren gumler:
da går ungdom til dans
på dit bud, sankte Hans!
ret som føllet og lammet, der frit over engen sig tumler.
da går ungdom til dans
på dit bud, sankte Hans!
ret som føllet og lammet, der frit over engen sig tumler.

Vi elsker vort land,
og med sværdet i hånd
skal hver udenvælts fjende beredte os kende,
men mod ufredens ånd
over mark, under strand
vil vi båler på fædrenes gravhøje tænde:
hver by har sin heks, og hvert sogn sine trolde,
vi vil fred her til lands
sankte Hans, sankte Hans!
den kan vindes, hvor hjerterne aldrig bli'r tvivlende kolde!
vi vil fred her til lands
sankte Hans, sankte Hans!
den kan vindes, hvor hjerterne aldrig bli'r tvivlende kolde!

3   She is referring to the mountain of Bloksbjerg, which is the home of witches in
    Danish mythology.
4   The custom until the 1800s was generally to have a live cat in the barrel during
    the festival itself, which would be let free after the barrel was beaten, if it did
    not die of shock. Fastelavn thus shared similarities with the old German festival
    practice of killing cats, sometimes by burying them alive, to ward off evil.

5   Witch effigies were a late addition to the Sankt Hans Eve celebrations, appearing in the early 1700s. Before this, Sankt Hans was believed to be a time of almost sacred power, which the natural world had absorbed from the sun during the long summer days (see also Hastrup 1985:28). For this reason, healers gathered herbs at this time and people drank, bathed in and slept next to springs all over the country. But the powers of evil were equally strong at this time, which is why the song speaks of the need to protect the land from the everpresent evil of witches and trolls. Neither Norway nor Sweden had the custom of burning a witch; the practice is closer to the German tradition, in which effigies of strawmen [strådukke] were burnt (Lindquist 2001).

6   I am grateful to Lise Skov for her remark that witchburning actually took place in Denmark after the country had been Christianized, and was practiced until 300 years ago. The first witchburning took place in 1540 and the last official witchburning took place in 1693, but there are records of women being pursecuted as witches up until WWI (Lindquist 2001).

7   Bakhtin (1968) has observed that at times of carnival, images of body life transgress ordinary social divisions and so create the grounds for a shared and universalized experience.

8   Bama is the word in this region for Aboriginal.

9   A hi-lux is an open-back four-wheel drive truck.

10 See Biddle (1991) for an account of the importance of the audience for the truth of stories among Walpiri. See also Myer's (1986) discussion of the relationship between the substance of public meetings among Pintupi and the will towards social consensus. Ochs and Capps illustrate that awareness of audience responsiveness creates ongoing subtle shifts in everyday storytelling in the US (Ochs and Capps 2001).

References

Ardener, Edwin 1992: Ritual og socialt rum. In: 'Ritualer', Tidsskriftet Antropologi 25, København: Foreningen Stofskifte: 23–28.

Asad, Talal 1973: Anthropology and the Colonial Encounter. London.

Bakhtin, Mikhail 1968. Rabelais and His World. Trans. Helene Iswolksy. Cambridge, Mass. the M.I.T. Press.

Bhabha, Homi K. 1994: The Location of Culture. Routledge: London and New York.

Baumann, Gerd 1996: Contesting Culture – Discourses of Identity in Multi-Ethnic London. Cambridge: Cambridge University Press.

Benjamin, Walter 1968: Illuminations. Trans. H. Zohn. New York: Harcourt, Brace, and World.

Biddle, Jennifer 1991: Dot, circle, difference: translating Central Desert paintings. In: Cartographies: Poststructuralism and the mapping of Bodies and Spaces. Ed. Rosalyn Diprose and Robyn Ferrell. Sydney. Allen and Unwin.

Damsholt, Tine 2000: Jeg ser de bøgelyse øer – og dette folk er vort. Om emotionalisering, subjektivering og danske sange. Tidsskriftet Antropologi Nr. 42: 49–67.

Devereux, George 1978: *Ethnopsychoanalysis*. Berkeley: University of California Press. 'Two types of modal personality models'. pp: 113–135.

Hastrup, Kirsten 1985: *Culture and History in Medieval Iceland. An anthropological analysis of structure and social change.* Oxford. Clarenden Press.

Hjemdahl, Kirsti Mathiesen 2003: *Tur/retur temapark – oppdragelse, opplevelse, kommers.* Kristiansand: Høyskoleforlaget.

Kristeva, Julia 1991: *Strangers to Ourselves*. New York. Columbia University Press. Trans. by Leon S. Roudiez.

Lindquist, Hanne D. 2001: Internet site: homeO.inet.tele.dk/damian/Hans

Myers, Fred 1996: 'Reflections on a meeting; structure, language, and the polity in a small-scale society.' In D. Brenneis and R.K.S. Macaulay (eds) *The Matrix of Language.* Boulder: Westview Press. pp: 234–257.

Ochs, Elinor and Capps, Lisa 2001: *Living Narrative. Creating Lives in Everyday Storytelling.* Cambridge, MA: Harvard University Press.

KIRSTI MATHIESEN HJEMDAHL

When Theme Parks Happen

Most research focuses on what theme parks *are*; how can they be defined, how typical they are compared to other forms of landscapes or cultural production. Not many cultural studies try to understand how they *happen*; focusing on what is actually taking place inside the theme parks and how the fairytales they tell come true.

I have been inspired by how a phenomenological approach has, so to speak, opened up the theme park in ways that neither ideological critique nor theories of modernity have done. Instead of standing on the sidelines, trying to work out what happens or does not happen within the theme park, I have thrown myself wholeheartedly into experiencing the potential of the fairytales, so that instead of trying to read the theme park culturally, I have tried to experience it culturally. With the help of Aksel, my research assistant who is six years old, I have come to some understanding of what they can be about.

This chapter deals with the experience of the theme parks, which can be separated into three phases: the first is where you are full of expectation, the second is where illusions are shattered, and the third is where magic moments can occur[1]. But before describing these experiences, I would like to comment briefly on the character of the theme parks and my own experiences as a researcher in these arenas of cultural production. How do you do fieldwork in the fairytale world of Moomins and Pippi Longstocking and among holidaymakers and children eating icecream?

Demanding Arenas for Cultural Production

Theme parks represent a demanding form of storytelling. Whereas you might have previously entered the world of fairytales from a certain distance – by listening to the radio, reading books, watching

TV, going to the cinema or the theatre – all these forms are now to be found in theme parks. By encountering the fairytale whilst seated, for example on a cosy lap, in a comfortable armchair, you are supposed to physically enter the landscape of the theme park. Rather than being led into the magic through narration, you move in and around this physical world of fairytales where you can create, enjoy, experience, re-experience and recognise. This is how the former children's ombudsman, Trond Viggo Torgersen, explains his first meeting with Cardemom Town in Kristiansand Theme park:

> As several other kids, I dreamt myself into the town and wondered what it would smell like there and what was around the corner of the drawings. Now I am 39 years old, and I have been in Cardemom Town. I have seen around the corners and slept in a bed there. It was almost unbelieveble, even though I was grown up and it was a normal bed. I think it was just like this Thorbjørn Egner wanted me to feel. Have this tickling, adventurous feeling of crawling into a drawing. Maybe the robbers are going to come. Maybe Aunt Sofie will sing a song. And when they did – because they did – I got almost the same feeling as just before unwrapping the presents on Christmas Eve when I was a little child (Egner 1992).

In the theme park, the fairytales concentrate on particular places in a landscape. The Moomin Park brochure invites you to 'Enter the fairytale. In Moomin Valley everything is absolutely true.' The same goes for the World of Astrid Lindgren, which constantly repeats the phrase 'Where fairytales become real'.

It is obvious that these claims represent a moderated truth as well as differing opinions of what really comes true within the world of the theme parks French researchers have likened EuroDisney to a cultural Chernobyl (Boniface and Fowler, 1993:148). 'An allegory of the consumer society, a place of absolute iconism, Disneyland is also a place of total passivity. Its visitors must agree to behave like its robots. Access to each attraction is regulated by a maze of metal railings which discourages any individual initiative', says Umberto Eco (1986:48). These are representative examples from cultural researchers who have visited theme parks. Some of them come to the same conclusions, proudly claiming that they have never been to a theme park at all (Dean MacCannel, 1992:74).

The philosopher, Edward Casey, says; 'Places not only are, they happen. And it is because they happen they lend themselves so well to narration, whether as history or as story' (Edward Casey, 1996:27). Through his understanding of place he indicates that the theme parks, through their placeness, at least have the potential to be good storytellers. But of course this transformation from place to the magical world of fairytales is not easy. The theme park puts whole landscapes on stage and tells several stories at the same time. The most important component needed to bring the fairytales alive seems to be based on something that is beyond the control of the parks: the visitors themselves. As I see it, they do not behave like robots at all.

While I can understand Eco's point about there being a lot of structure in the parkscapes telling us where and how to move, it is probably not surprising that I disagree because I do not think that he can have spent much time moving around within the theme-parks with children.

In order for a researcher to understand how fairytales can come true, I think that it is nessasary to base an analysis of the theme parks which opens up so much more than a structural reading. Edward Casey's understanding of place is much more than just the structural and semiotic; 'The primacy of place is not that of the place, much less of this place or a place (not even a very special place) – all these locations imply place-as-simple-presence – but that of being an event capable of implacing things in many complex manners and to many complex effects', he says. Casey does not consider place as a physical 'container', but as the most fundamental form of bodily experience; 'Given that we are never without perception, the existence of this dialectic means that we are never without emplaced experiences. It signifies as well that we are not only in places but of them' (Casey, 1996:19). The author Albert Camus helps us even further in approaching the theme park in a different way, by underlining that: 'Sense of place is not just something that people know and feel, it is something people do' (in Basso, 1996:83).

I am convinced that theme parks represent extremely demanding forms of storytelling and cultural production precisely because it is the doing that is essential in the effort of making fairytales come true within them. You have to be capable of, and willing to, climb into – and also maybe onto – the fairytales in order to make them happen. You could possibly say that you *do* a theme park, rather than you *are* in a theme park.

Even though the parks depend on people's participation in order to happen, the visitors are dependent on the storytelling of the parkscape itself. The parks function like diving boards for the imagination. The stories that are being told in the theme park are to be found within the designing and building of the setting, as much as in the particular performances. Therefore when entering the theme parks you profit from pre-knowledge. During a day in the park, you are likely to meet the fairytales more in the form of silent stages rather than performing actors. To make fairytales happen, you have to be able to fill the houses and settings with meaning and excitement yourself, to allow them to do the telling and moving, and to have the energy to continue seeking if the fairytale does not happen at a particular moment.

Fairytales are not told from the beginning to a 'happily ever after' end, but are performed in terms of highlights, both on stage and by random meetings. The ability to improvise and interact with the audience is perhaps the biggest advantage when compared to other forms of storytelling. To understand the rapid performances, to be able to join in and contribute to the spontanity of improvisation, you need to know both the characters and the context of the stories. However, you are by no means dependent on them but much more dependent upon the will and ability to imagine and participate.

Theme parks are often considered to be prototypes of the hyper-real, postmodern worlds of imagination, where scenes of pleasure and fantasy are more real than reality itself (Baudrillard 1988, Urry 1990, Featherstone 1991, Zukin 1992, Eco 1986). The strong claims of authenticity that the parks build upon (i.e. here everything is absolutely true), make the park adventure an even more demanding form of storytelling than a book, a film or the theatre. In addition, the theme park tour is so much more than just meeting the adventure; families are supposed to have a friendly and exciting 'holiday of their dreams' together. And of course, there are commercial stories to be told as well. Several tales are supposed to become true during a day in the theme park.

It is very easy to get lost in this multidimensional form of storytelling. Many things can distract and disturb the potential magical moments. The parks therefore put a lot of effort into explaining, guiding, and helping visitors with signs, maps and suggestions of suitable routes through the landscape. In the most professional parks you receive updated information about how long you have to stand in a queue before reaching the attraction. Most cultural researchers have focused on this overwhelming amount of information and guiding, often with a negative outcome (Hjemdahl, 1995:7–11). Cultural identity is left with few options in the carefully controlled surroundings (Eco 1986, Wilson 1992), or leads to the end of the social (Baudrillard 1888).

This critical thinking, which is focused on ideologies, has itself been critisised by cultural researchers at the Center of Contemporary Cultural Studies (CCCS) in Birmingham UK (Willis 1990, Fiske 1989, Laermans 1992) and also by modern theorists such as Melucci (1991), Giddens (1991), Featherstone (1991) and Marcus (1992). More optimistic thinking has not really contributed with further knowledge about how the tales come true. Despite the understanding of theme park consumption as a liberating force and an arena for personal creativity and heterogenic forces, ethnographic studies have tended to focus more on the symbols rather than the experience, and on the response more than the doing, thus giving cultural identity more possibilities than might otherwise have been the case (Hjemdahl 1995). It is easy to feel as if you are drifting through a symbolic wood or exposed to meanings and tellings, as Orvar Löfgren (1993) puts it, where all alternative uses of the surroundrings are seen as examples of cultural resistance.

Phenomenological Entrance to the Theme Park

Turning towards a phenomenological way of thinking has helped me to focus more on *how* the fairytales come true in the parks. In short, that means being in the park just as you are meant to be there – participating and experiencing.

The work of Jonas Frykman (1999) shows that such phenomenologically inspired research is more oriented towards practical knowledge rather than that which is cognitive. It emphasises the accidental and the local more than the national and the global, and puts experience before theory. A phenomenological approach is an enquiry into the potentials of experience – a knowledge that is prediscursive. The anthroplogist Michael Jackson decribes it like this:

> Phenomenology is the scientific study of experience. It is an attempt to describe human consciousness in its lived immediacy, before it is subject to theoretical elaboration or conceptual systemizing … Rather than examine the epistemological status of beliefs it is more important to explore their existential uses and consequences. Our emphasis is thus shifted from what beliefs 'mean' *intrinsically* to what they are made to mean, and what they accomplish for those who invoke and use them. (Jackson, 1996:2–6).

The way that I do fieldwork in the parks is strongly inspired by Michael Jackson's thinking on practical mimesis, or 'thinking with one's feet' (Jackson, 1996:28–29). To participate bodily in the practical doings of everyday life, using the body as others do, is a creative and rewarding methodological technique that grasps the meaning connected to different doings, experiences and expressions, as well as putting practices and reflections into context. Jackson (1983:340) says that to stand beside the action, to gather opinions and to ask endless questions, raises the phenomenological problem about how to understand the experience of others.

From my fieldwork I have also learnt to see how the parks change character. I have done two theme park tours through the Nordic landscape – visiting Moomin Valley in Finland, Astrid Lindgren's World in Sweden, Legoland in Denmark and Cardamom Town in

Kristiansand Zoo, Norway. There was an enormous difference in the ways I understood and experienced the parks when I visited them in 1996 and when I visited them again two years later.

The first time I travelled alone, and above all felt lonely, especially as many people were visiting in groups. I interviewed and observed a lot of people, both guests and those involved in managing the parks. In short, I tried to experience the parks through other people. But a day in the theme park is not arranged in such a way that people want (or can endure) to have a curious ethnologist following at their heels. Most people spend one day (or a maximum of two) on what is considered to be the biggest adventure of the summer, and they are often busy relating to the different wants and needs within the family. Even though I turned up at the very moment the families had a rest, ate their lunch, or just relaxed while the kids continued their adventures, my way into the park-experience was reduced to dialogues about the experiences before and after the real happenings.

Of course I entered the fairytales myself, and had fun on my own by looking in the houses, talking to the fairytale characters and enjoying the acting and improvisations. I tried the 'don't-step-on-the-ground'-trial in Astrid Lindgren's World, entered the competitions along Toffle's path in Moomin Valley, sang along to 'You're not supposed to believe it's summer', steered the pirate ship of Captain Dagger tooth in Kristiansand Zoo and so on.

Despite this involvement, I still found myself on the periphery of the big events. I had most of my greatest moments on the lawn in front of Moomin House with a cup of coffee in one hand, an ice cream in the other, and with a panoramic view over the heart of the park. In the theme park-genre it is often called Kodak Picture point, as it is where things happen. I could have spent hours on that lawn, watching the children playing with, hugging and saying hello to the Moomins. In Astrid Lindgren's World there was an even greater repertoire of settings where I could follow the acting via the interactive scenes with the audience, and follow the crowds of people coming and going. But even so, I still did not feel that I had really got hold of the parks.

I did not realise how little I had actually grasped of the happenings before I travelled to the parks the second time, together with six-year-old Aksel, his mother and a friend. I had told my companions about the nice lawn in front of Moomin House and I was looking forward to enjoying, watching, commenting upon and experiencing the world of Moomins again, this time in company.

During the five days' stay in Moomin Valley, we sat on the lawn for approximately 30 minutes. There was neither the time nor the potential for more because every time something happened in front of us, we had to join in. We had to say hello, play, hug, go through Moomin House once more, check again if anyone had entered the house of Hemulen, or find out if Stinky had been arrested again. The theme park had a totally different rhythm and speed. From the calm, harmonic, somewhat laidback if controlled atmosphere that I had experienced when being alone (which corresponded to how the parks presented themselves), the parks took a character of stress, high pulse, confusion and almost aggressiveness. But at the same time the parks were more exciting and challenging to be in. The shift of speed took form in other ways too.

You do not walk quietly among the attractions with a six-year-old. You run, especially around Toffle's path in Moomin World. When Aksel ran he was full of enthusiasm, questioning, commenting, paying attention and experiencing. I followed at his heels, with the tape recorder running so that I could concentrate fully on his meeting with the materiality of the tales. Anna followed us with her camera and Martin brought up the rear, carrying all our bags and belongings. When Aksel had completed the first round of the path, he immediately wanted to do it again. And again. After a while we grown ups started taking turns to follow Aksel. He just could not get enough, and he did not lose his eagerness either. There were new things to discover, and old things to rediscover.

Through this micro-ethnographic fieldwork, I came to a totally different understanding about how theme parks happen, how they speak and move, and how you get in touch with their senses. The first thing that Aksel showed me was how important fantasy is as a power to make the park happen and how this runs through several phases.

As I see it, Aksel's first meeting with 'the real, true' Moomin Valley, can also be regarded as the first phase in the experience of the theme park; filled with expectation and with an open and positive mind, he ran into the fairytale where everything is absolutely true.

First Phase – Full of Expectations

Aksel wipes his shoes conscientiously on the broom placed by the entrance of Moomin House. You certainly do not tramp through the house with dirty shoes when you visit the Moomin Family. 'You didn't do it', points out the boy who does not usually concern himself with matters of hygiene. He waits patiently on the veranda until my sandals are also free from sand and mud.

It does not take Aksel long to scan the ground floor, before he runs eagerly towards the stairs. 'Are you finished already?' I ask, thinking he has been rather quick. 'Yes, there's not much to see down there', Aksel replies positively. Moomin House is not that interesting when the family is not there. As he climbs the stairs to the first floor he asks expectantly, 'Do you think this is going to be fun?' I remember that the first time we passed through Moomin House, the Snorkmaiden sat in her chair relaxing, while she waved to all the children staring from the other side of the rope barriers. The second time was a complete flop as there were not any Moomin figures at all. It looks as if that might be the case this time too; 'I can't see anyone. There's no one here now', he says disappointed after completing his exploration of the first floor. But after only a few seconds, he is again filled with optimism. 'Then they'll have to be on the next floor'. We continue to climb the stairs.

'Who's that, sitting there?' I ask, really pleased and almost relieved.

'Moominpappa', he answers happily, as he gets to see Moominpappa sitting by the typewriter in his study. His stick is beside the table, and his big black hat hangs on the hat-and-coat stand.

'Yes, is he sitting there writing?' I wonder. It is apparently so, because it is not difficult to work out that this Moominpappa is just an empty shell. The bulky costume is placed in the chair, and to keep the balance, his big Moomin head leans on the typewriter. But Aksel is not that interested in what Moominpappa is doing. He wants contact.

'Hiiiiiiii', he shouts, 'Hi Moomipappa'. Moominpappa does not react at all. He does not answer or wave back.

'I think he's concentrating. You see he's sitting with his nose on the typing keys', I say, almost apologising for Moominpappa's lack of interest towards the engaged and excited boy.

'Hi Moominpappa, hi', he tries again, before he says disappointedly: 'He's not coming. He's never coming'.

'No, maybe he's writing a new novel', I say in an attempt to rescue the situation.

'He's not writing', Aksel correctly points out. No, of course he is not. His hands just lie there in his lap, without moving.

'Maybe he's thinking of a new novel', I try, beginning to find the whole situation rather unpleasant. I cannot tell him, or can I? I suppose I just hope that Aksel will soon want to continue to climb up the stairs, searching for new members of the Moomin Family.

'There's a picture of him. Isn't he funny?' Aksel laughs and looks at the beautifully framed picture of Moominpappa in his black beret, hanging on the wall.

'Yes, he's a bit funny', I admit.

'But I wonder why he's sitting there concentrating so hard?' asks Aksel, somewhat disgruntled although not totally displeased: 'Where's the camera?' he asks.

'Hi Moominpappa, hi', he shouts again, hoping that Moominpappa might manage to tear himself away from whatever he is doing. 'Do you think he remembers me?'

'Yes, you met him yesterday, didn't you?'

'Yes.'

'Well, maybe', I suggest carefully, and then ask, 'do you think he remembers you?'

'Hey, why is this sitting straight up like this?' Aksel asks while fumbling with the rope separating us from Moominpappa's room. It seems as if he is finished with Moominpappa for the time being. He walks towards the stairs. 'Moomintroll is upstairs. Maybe some of the others are there too? Maybe Snorkmaiden is there?' he says with renewed optimism as we begin climbing the stairs to the third floor.

Moomintroll is not on the third floor, and neither is Snorkmaiden nor any other character from the Moomin Family. But about one thousand million other people are also looking for them, or at least, that is what it feels like. They are all queuing up to go down the narrow stairs leading to the cellar. That is what Aksel wants to do too, because he is convinced that is where Stinky is. I try to argue that it is far less painful to go back the way we came, but Aksel has made up his mind: 'No, we go down this way, because the cellar is down there and that's where Stinky is. Stanky, I mean. Stanky', he laughs. He continues to talk to himself. 'Stinky, Stanky, Stanky. Come on, Stanky. Come on. Come again, Stinky, where are you?' But he rather quickly turns his attention back towards his environment; 'More and more people are arriving. No one's going down. Hey, they are jumping the queue. Why are they jumping the queue? We can do that as well!'

'No, we can't', I say, stepping into the serious role of the responsible adult.

'She's jumping the queue', he says again, loudly, clearly and totally correctly.

After a while we begin to do the same! We circle down, down and down the stairs. Of course there is no Stinky in the basement, and to be honest I am feeling quite disappointed by this trip through Moomin House. First and foremost I am disappointed for Aksel. It should be possible to make sure that at least one member of the Moomin family is in the house all the time – someone to return all the enthusiastic waves. You would also think that it would relieve some of the pressure on the little gravelled terrace just outside Moomin House, where the Moomins almost continuously replace each other. But Aksel is feeling far more uplifted then I am when we come out into the sunshine again and hear the ever present background Moomin music 'mamma-mamma-mamma-mamma-mamma, pappa-pappa-pappa-pappa-pappa-pappa-pappa, mamma-mamma-mamma, pappa-pappa-pappa-pappa'. And then he gets his reward. After several disappointments, the star of Moomin Valley appears.

'Here's Stinky. Come on', I say, feeling pleased.

'Yes, Hahira', laughs Aksel while running to look at the funny, black, almost square formed Stinky. 'Look, he's staring at me. He's staring straight at me. Ha-ha-ha', laughs Aksel enthusiastically. 'Does he stink?' he asks.

'Could you smell something?'

'No', Aksel says. He couldn't.

'Maybe he's been washed', I suggest.

'Maybe he's been arrested again?' suggests Aksel, remembering what happens to Stinky in Moomin Valley. Stinky escapes from prison, is arrested by the Moomin Police and then escapes again on his way back to prison, but then gets caught again after running through the crowd of people. The Moomin Police always accompany Stinky. He needs company, because the children are not particularly nice to him. They hit and push and pull him. But Stinky is not particularly nice either.

'Did you see that? Look. He-he-he-he. Isn't he cool', laughs Aksel, really pleased. Stinky turns toward a child who is trying to touch him – not to hug and put his arms around the child's shoulders which is the usual position for having a photograph taken, but he hisses while lifting his arms threateningly, as if he is going to capture the child.

'He's just mega cool. He walks so fast. Stinky walks so fast. Do you think Stinky is going to fall in love with Snorkmaiden?' Aksel makes small talk as he runs beside Stinky. Stinky constantly pushes and pulls the children swarming around him.

'Smell, smell. Did you see that? Did he start to shove? Are you going to say hi to him? Say hi to him'. For a moment I am almost more excited than Aksel because here is the golden opportunity of real contact with Stinky.

'Ugh', Aksel exclaims as he gets close to Stinky's black body.

'Did he smell?' I ask, fascinated about what you can imagine if only the will is strong enough. Or are they really so professional in the Moomin Valley that they inject a horrible smell into Stinky's costume?

'Yes, he smelled really bad'

'Oh, then I'm glad I didn't get to smell him. I've got a very sensitive sense of smell, you know.'

'Do you want do know what he smelled like?' Aksel asks.

'What did he smell like?'

'He smelled like garbage.'

The Second Phase – The Shattering of Illusions

After the tour of Moomin House and the encounter with Stinky, we sit down on the lawn to cool down with an ice cream. We watch the array of people and Moomintroll, and Aksel tells Anna and Martin what we have experienced; that he has met Moominpappa, that Snorkmaiden wore a nice pearl necklace, and that Stinky smelled of garbage. We watch closely to see who comes out of the little house near Moomin House (which we grown-ups understand is a dressing room, although Aksel does not know that – although he knows that there is no such house in Moomin Valley). Aksel runs down to hug and say hello to each figure that comes out. Suddenly something weird happens. 'Look, why does Moominpappa come out of that house when he's sitting in Moomin House writing?' asks Aksel, 'It must have been a Cheating Moominpappa at the typewriter'. He turns around and shouts, as runs down to hug the one he has just identified as the real Moominpappa. When he joins us again, he will not let this go. He wants to go into Moomin House again, to check if the Cheating Moominpappa is still sitting there. Luckily we manage to distract him with one more ice cream and another round of Toffle's path. The undeniable evidence of cheating threatens the magic of the theme park. It must keep some of the mystique. As with Santa Claus, you know deep down that he does not exist, but you are not really sure. At least that is what we think.

The parks set high goals when they invite people into the reality of the fairytales. On many levels, theme parks are at the mercy of amateurs; part time workers, young employees, summer replacements of Pippi, student Moomins, and depend on economics rather than culture when seen from the eyes of the management. In addition, the lack of distance between the stage and the audience does not only highlight but also reveals. One can claim that it is impossible to physically rebuild the imaginative stories that are being told in the books and films. Crowds of young fairytale connoisseurs enter the theme parks and they are very specific and detail-oriented in their expectations with regard to the settings, the characters and the stories. Perhaps that is why the second phase in the theme park experience takes the form of an illusion, often filled with disappointment.

It is as if the missing links are all you can see – everything that is not true. On Toffle's path, Aksel shatters one illusion after the other: We do not have to worry about the bats, because they are only plastic. It is not dangerous if we fall into the waterfall, because it is shallow and made of blue and green glass fibre. The mist rising from the screen does not prove that Hufsa has recently passed by, because the smoke really comes from a cable underneath the stones. The trees in the whispering wood do not really whisper, because when you look into the trees it is easy to see the loudspeakers. Any final doubt is cleared away when we hear the jarring sound from worn out loudspeakers.

You might ask why the ideal of total authenticity is regarded as being so important. Why is it so difficult for the parks or the parents to tell the kids that actors play the part of Moomins, Pippi and the others – and because they are so good at it, that they actually become Moomins and Pippi? Theatre manages to do this, without breaking the illusions. Is it because the children's naivety is regarded as something pure and holy and almost of religious dimension or that the children's fantasy is destroyed if they know too much? Do we presume that a good childhood includes having believed in Santa Claus, because if that is the case then it is even worse when the parks do not deliver the perfect illusion?

Often the parks do not manage to live up to their promises of being the places where fairytales become absolutely true. Sometimes they even make it far too easy for eager children – and likewise difficult for parents who have actually decided to enter the world of fairytales. The ideal of not revealing that someone is behind the masks of the fairytale characters falls flat when the park does not manage to supervise how many Moominpappas appear in the park at the same time, and when the zips on the backs of the Moomin costumes are obvious for everyone with their eyes open to see, or when the person inside Hemulen becomes visible through the flashlights and camera lenses. At the same time, the eagerness for authenticity takes a somewhat peculiar form when a seven-year-old girl is employed as Little My. She might be the same size as her character, but when she turns her back towards the visitors to Moomin Valley because of shyness, the potential for bringing the fairytale to life is reduced. The result is the most introverted Little My the world has ever seen.

It is often the little things that seem to be out of place. For example, it is important to make sure that Hufsa's outfit covers the wheels of the small board that rolls her on stage, so that we do not have to close our eyes to imagine how she moves through the landscape in her usual, motionless way. One should also be aware that at the end of the show, at least twenty children will run down to look behind the curtain to make sure that Hufsa was actually sent back to the woods before she was zoomed back to her ordinary size. It would therefore be a good idea to hide the large Hufsa from these curious children, who most of all want to believe what they have been presented with on stage. When you invite children to play in the fairytales, you also have to see to it that the most important elements are present. For instance, when you crawl under Bertil's bed, to visit Nils Karlsson Pyssling inside the rat hole, the nail should really be in place so that saying 'Killevippen' really is magic. Otherwise how can you become small enough, like in the actual story?

In such cases, it seems that the will and ability to imagine and dream is really being challenged.

Third Phase – The Will and Ability to Imagine

The philosopher Gaston Bachelard says that it is the literary and the virtual that give ground to Goethe's dynamic masochism: 'It's hardly any real pleasure other than in the moment where fraud begins' (Bachelard, 1992:328). The ethnologist Orvar Löfgren (1990:8) claims that deconstructing the hunt for the authentic and displaying its shallowness or artificiality belongs to an old tradition.

Deconstructing the fairytale is also part of a learning process; one learns how to direct the look, to see the place as it *is*. When you first see the chicken wire and the zips, you also learn that things do not have their own life and do not carry any magic. Teaching yourself not to imagine – not to be struck by the mystique – and instead seeing things only as they *are* is a learning process in itself. 'It's not about looking closely, but dreaming hard', says Bachelard (1992:23). He is concerned with creative imagination rather than reproduction and that the indistinct is at least as productive as the distinct. If something is too clear and obvious, it serves to block the imagination (Bachelard, 2000:159).

Bachelard is occupied with the thoughts and images that are received, created and produced rather than the things themselves. He praises artists who are rather uninteresting as artists, but who have nevertheless given him dreams and thoughts. Bachelard's reasoning on dreams is therefore more concerned about how the material, the artefacts, the place and the things cannot be given significance as objects, but as subjects. In other words, how they act upon us, and how we discover new parts of ourselves through dreaming about them.

When the objects are obvious as in the theme parks and so easy to reveal, some people worry that a trip to the theme park will be one of disillusion and demystification and that the joy of imagination will be taken away from children too quickly and too easily.

One might underestimate both the ability and willingness of children to imagine, because they are ready to compensate. Aksel was much more willing to give the theme park a second chance than I had either the ability or the will to.

The journey to the theme park is not only a project of revealing, where one is occupied with finding the things that confirm that the fairytale is not absolutely true. On the contrary, it was fascinating to see how Aksel's enthusiasm redefined the first disappointment into something he could still enter into and get involved with. The ability and will to imagine is what gives form to the third phase in the process of making the theme park's tales come true: the place is re-enchanted, and again becomes a spring board for the imagination.

Even if Aksel discovered that Toffle's path was plastic, it did not discourage him from further investigation. With enormous enthusiasm he continued to run through the path at least twice a day. He wanted the tales to be true – so much so that when an extra Moominpappa turned up, the first one was immediately regarded as a fake, while the other one was real: 'I have to go down and say hello to the real Moomin Papa'.

Maybe the theme park does much more than shatters illusions. Does it deal with complex understandings of reality or hyper-realities? It gives you a special feeling to sit in the cinema on Trouble-maker Street and watch the movie 'Lotta on Troublemaker Street', with your arm wrapped tightly around Lotta's bear, just like Lotta herself is doing in the movie. The fact that the bear is actually a pink pig seems natural. The same goes for Astrid Lindgren's World. Even if Karlsson on the Roof did not fly, Aksel was very pleased when he discovered how he could have done it: 'I discovered how Karlsson on the Roof's propeller works. He pushes the big, white button in the front of his pants!' And even though Mattis Castle was not a real castle, it still was fun to play inside. It is even more fun when the area is filled with Mattis robbers and Borka robbers, who do not only act but also start fighting and competing with all the knights. Perhaps the theme park contributes to creative imagination and the ability to dream without scrutinising everything too closely.

Sometimes you are fortunate enough to experience magic moments, like we did one Sunday afternoon in Moomin Valley. It is our fifth and last day in the park, and there is only an hour left before it closes so there are not many people left. Moomintroll is sitting on the little bridge outside Moomin House. Aksel sits close to him, almost hidden from view in the big, white Moomin body. He holds the troll's hand firmly and at the same time pats Moomintroll on the hand and knee and caresses his huge nose. Sometimes he just closes his eyes and leans into the soft body. What bliss!

Beside him sits a little boy called Emil, who is also a fan. He is wearing a blue, home knitted sweater with a white Moomintroll clearly visible on his chest. Repeatedly he asks, 'Moomin, do you want me to kill the Hattifatterner for you? Moomin, do you want me to kill the Hattifatterner for you? Moomin, Moomin. Moomin, do you want me to kill the Hattifatterner for you?' He runs back and forth, muttering that he now has killed the Hattifatterner, and the same time asks again whether he should do it. Moomintroll does not answer, because the troll is not allowed to talk when he is in the park. He can only talk when he is on stage.

Aksel enjoys everything – the hugs, pats and caresses. A small yellow, plastic fish swims by under the bridge. 'That was the fish Stinky tried to catch when he was put in jail', Aksel comments. Moomintroll nods, and pats him on the head, as if he is saying 'that's right, my boy'. The two on the bridge manage to talk, even if not with words. Then it happens. Moomintroll leans towards Aksel. The boy's eyes widen and he opens his mouth.

'He talked. Moomintroll talked to me!' he shouts.

'What did he say?' we ask from the other side of the pond.

'Moomin loves you.'

Aksel keeps repeating these delicious words as he leans closer to Moomintroll. For those of us standing around watching, this is almost as magic as it is for the main character. This is the moment you hope for, in the place where fairytales come true.

Moomintroll and Aksel sit together until it is time to close the park. When we are gathering our things to leave, Moomintroll approaches me. He probably thinks that I am the boy's mother, because of all the photographs I have taken of the two on the bridge. He leans towards me, and articulates something that would warm every parent's heart: 'What a wonderful child'. When I tell this to Aksel later on, his body totally relaxes. He smiles, but also looks somewhat embarrassed. The feeling of happiness is almost too much for a six-year-old boy.

Notes

1   This chapter is part of my PhD thesis on Nordic Literary Theme parks; the Kristiansand Theme park in Norway, with Cardamom Town and the World of Captain Daggertooth, Moomin World in Finland, and the World of Astrid Lindgren in Sweden. In my thesis I focus on why so many families consider theme parks to be cultural necessities, what one actually does in the theme park, which elements appear in everyday life, and how theme park culture is produced.

References

Bachelard, Gaston 1992: *Jorden och viljans drömmerier*. Lund: Skarabé.
Bachelard, Gaston 2000: *Rummets poetik*. Lund: Skarabé.

Basso, Keith H. 1996: Wisdom Sits in Places: Notes on a Western Apache Landscape. In: Feld, Steven and Keith H. Basso (eds): *Senses of Place*, pp: 53–90.

Baudrillard, Jean 1988: *Selected Writings*. Cambridge and Oxford: Polity Press and Basil Blackwell.

Boniface, Pricilla and Peter J. Fowler 1993: *Heritage and Tourism in 'the Global Village'*. London and New York: Routledge.

Casey, Edward 1996: How to Get From Space to Place in a Fairly Short Stretch of Time: Phenomenological Prolegomena. In: Feld, Steven & Keith. H. Basso (eds): *Senses of Place*. Santa Fe: School of American Research Press.

Eco, Umberto 1986: *Travels in Hyperreality*. San Diego, New York, London: Harcourt Brace Jovanovich, Publishers.

Egner, Bjørn 1992: *Kardemomme by i Kristiansand Dyrepark*. Oslo: J.W. Cappelens Forlag AS.

Featherstone, Mike 1991: *Consumer Culture & Postmodernism*. London, Newbury Park, New Dehli: SAGE Publications.

Fiske, John 1989: *Understanding Popular Culture*. Boston: Unwin Hyman

Frykman, Jonas 1999: Hem til Europa. Platser för identitet och handling. *RIG* nr 2, pp: 81–94.

Giddens, Anthony 1992: *Modernity and Self-Identity. Self and Society in the Late Modern Age*. Cambridge: Polity Press.

Hjemdahl, Kirsti Mathiesen 1995: *Der eventyr blir virkelighet På kulturanalytisk oppdagelsesferd i et dyreparklandskap*. IKK: hovedfagsoppgave.

Hjemdahl, Kirsti Mathiesen 2003: *Tur-retur temapark – oppdragelse, opplevelse, kommers*. Kristiansand: Høyskoleforlaget.

Jackson, Michael 1983: Knowledge of the body. *Man* (N.S) 18, pp: 327–345.

Jackson, Michael 1996: Introduction: Phenomenology, Radical Empiricism, and Anthropological Critique. In: Michael Jackson (ed). *Things as They are. New Directions in Phenomenological Anthropology*. Bloomington and Indianapolis: Indiana University Press.

Laermans, Rudi 1992: Bringing the Consumer Back in. *Theory, Culture & Society*, Vol 10 nr 1, pp: 153–161.

Löfgren, Orvar 1990: Consuming Interests. *Culture & History* 7, pp: 7–36.

Löfgren, Orvar 1993: Are We Having Fun Yet? Approaches to the Cultural Analysis of Consumption. *Opening Note Presented at the Fourth Conference on Research in Consumption*, Amsterdam.

MacCannell Dean 1992: *Empty Meeting Grounds. The Tourist Papers*. London and New York: Routledge.

Marcus, Georg 1992: Past, Present and Emerging Identities. In: Scott Lash & Jonathan Friedman (eds). *Modernity and Identity*. Oxford UK & Cambridge USA: Blackwell.

Melucci, Alberto 1991: *Nomader i nuet. Sociala rörelser och individuella behov i dagens samhälle*. Göteborg: Daidalos.

Urry, John 1990: *The Tourist Gaze Leisure and Travel in Contemporary Societies*. London, Newbury Park, New Dehli: SAGE Publications.

Willis, Paul 1990: *Common Culture Symbolic Work at Play in the Everyday Cultures of the Young*. Milton Keynes: Open University Press.

Wilson, Alexander 1992: *The Culture of Nature. North American Landscape from Disney to the Exxon Valdez.* Cambridge MA & Oxford UK: Blackwell.

Zukin, Sharon 1992: Postmodern Urban Landscapes: Mapping Culture and Power. In: Scott Lash, & Jonathan Friedman (eds). *Modernity and Identity*, pp: 221–247. Oxford UK & Cambridge USA: Blackwell.

KJELL HANSEN

The Sensory Experience of Doing Fieldwork in an 'Other' Place

> We must not, therefore, wonder whether we really perceive a world,
> we must instead say: the world is what we perceive.
>
> Merleau-Ponty, 1999:xvi

This article describes a methodological experiment in ethnological fieldwork. As the experiment was not completely successful, it is not my intention to present it as a fully workable alternative to the more established research methods. However, I do believe that the experiment will serve to highlight some of the problems involved in changing our concepts about and attitudes towards what we consider to be 'proper' fieldwork.

The Problem with Fieldwork

In the introduction to a book that discusses the role of location in social anthropology, Akhil Gupta and James Ferguson (1997) have pointed to the fact that never before has the idea of 'fieldwork' had such an important impact on the discipline. I would claim that the same argument is also applicable to the discipline of European ethnology. In Scandinavia, the methodology of ethnographic fieldwork is being used as *the* point of distinction between social anthropology/European ethnology on the one hand, and disciplines such as human geography, history and sociology on the other.[1] The way we build our empirical base from being 'out there' – that is, in the field with ordinary people – has become a way of giving our disciplines their identities. We tend to become researchers that see ourselves as those who (claim to) know what the world really *is* like. This has established direct, personal experience in the field as the hallmark of good research. It would not be unreasonable to claim that 'doing fieldwork' today plays an important part in the identity construction of the discipline as such.

The common way for ethnologists to carry out their fieldwork is to go somewhere, usually not too far away, to find people to talk to (interview), and generally try to get some kind of impression of the actual setting.[2] Courses in methodology usually stress the importance of making tape recordings of the interviews, and transcribing all the details. If an interview has not been recorded, its value as a reliable source is effectively reduced, so that when referring to it in a text, one usually feels the need to argue its value and explain why it is being used. Other aspects of human actions, such as gestures, ways of doing things, clothing etc, are normally treated with much less accuracy.

Our present practices rely heavily on words and this can be traced back to the idea of fieldwork as a pure collecting of material. The early ethnologists set out to record the facts about previous lives and communities through old people's recollections of the past and usually linked to the collecting of artefacts. Such people were called informants and their narratives were seen as a direct link to the past, with the main source-critical question centring on the functions (or, rather, malfunctions) of memory. Once the narrative had been established as something other than pure imagination, it could – and would – be used as an example of a general, though usually geographically limited, phenomenon.

This point of view was strongly criticised during the latter part of the 20th century, and was finally defeated through what has been called 'the linguistic turn' that reached ethnology in the last quarter of the century. To put it bluntly, one could argue that the basic ideological idea of this perspective was that the world was a text, or rather, that we could not have any knowledge about the world other than linguistically. As social and cultural beings, we live in a world of narratives – both great and small – that constitute our perspective and understanding. This meant that the focus on words was retained in our methodology, despite the shift from seeing people's stories as possible presentations of a past or present real world, to seeing them as a source that enabled us to understand how people made sense of their worlds through language. Culture came to be seen as something that is constantly (re)created and changed, but which is primarily concerned with ways of thinking and patterns of values (cp. Ehn 1993:7f). So it is easy to see that the two positions are opposites, although they do have the common denominator of a profound trust in words as *the* main carrier of meaning for any ethnologist doing fieldwork. At best, other experiences are considered to be complementary, but are seldom seen to have any value in themselves.

Another aspect of this is that fieldwork has long since ceased to be regarded as a mere production of descriptions. Rather, in the last decades, ethnography has tended to become a discipline of clarification and interpretation. This, however, is seldom made transparent in published works. It is by no means unusual that researchers take personal experience as a starting point, but more often than not, they also tend to do nothing more than use it to sketch a situation and then quickly move on to more comprehensive interpretations (cp. Ehn 1993). In reality, of course, most of our interpretations of field material are based on inferences, in which we use knowledge gained outside the field situation to try to explain that which lies outside the original situation. One reason for this might be that today our lifeworlds are crisscrossed by references to things outside our everyday lives. One could probably say that what has happened in the late modern world is not so much that everyday *actions* have become more complex, but rather that *contexts* have become more difficult to survey (Hansen 2001). This naturally makes it hard to stick to the lifeworld situations that we meet in the field. Since words are our main reference source, it is often easy to put them into a world context, thereby missing the challenge of understanding how new contexts influence our day-to-day duties.

One of the aims of the experiment discussed in this article was to turn the habitual way of doing fieldwork upside-down: I wanted to test what might come from a situation in which the fieldworker consciously chose to abstain from talking to people, and instead relied on other sensory impulses. By concentrating on these other kinds of input and how it might be possible to use them to analyse an event, I also wanted to increase the transparency about how we actually make cultural interpretations in 'the field'.

Finding My Way

When we at the department of European Ethnology in Lund started to take the 'European' in our name seriously, and thus to conduct studies abroad, we suddenly found ourselves in circumstances that were new to us. To start with, we did not know very much (at least comparatively) about the societies in which we were doing fieldwork, and secondly, we often had great linguistic problems. One solution could have been to use the more traditional, social anthropological ways of conducting fieldwork, namely to stay in the field for at least a year and to learn the language. However, this proved to be impossible due to the costs involved, especially when research funding was diminishing. This was the harsh reality that led us to try to develop another kind of fieldwork. In this case, I wanted to test a lead, which I believe may be found in research inspired by phenomenology, namely to focus on the role of perception in establishing field material.

The central nub of my experiment was to put myself in a situation and then use my own reactions to it as the key to understanding what was taking place. It thus became important to be acutely attentive to the sensory impressions that were released in the situation, and to consciously test the limits of my own stock of experiences as a tool for understanding them. I used this method in a series of small fieldwork exercises, which formed the basis of an article entitled *Festivals, spatiality and the new Europe* (Hansen 2002). 'The fields' included a couple of local fairs, the celebration of two national commemoration days, and an open-air museum. My main methodological aim was to capture the experiences of being both a visitor and a participant in the events.

It was my participation in the celebration of Hungary's national holiday that changed what had just been a vague idea of 'taking part and being there', into a more profound method. Now, in discussing the method, I will therefore concentrate on what happened in Budapest during that early spring day in 1998.[3]

I had arrived the evening before the celebration was to take place and spent the night at one of the old, formerly fashionable, hotels on the Buda side of the city. A few days previously, someone had told me about the celebrations scheduled for Saturday, and I therefore traveled from Pècs, where I had been staying. On waking up, I was eager to go out and see what was going on. I do not know exactly what I expected, but on entering the hotel's dining room for breakfast, I felt disappointed. There was no sign of a celebration. It could just have been any ordinary Saturday. A little less eagerly, and certainly with diminished expectations, I crossed the bridge and headed towards the main street. On my way there, I did not see many indications that this was an important day for the nation – a flag here and there and a couple of people in their Sunday best – but nothing definite. It was not until I turned a corner, that I found myself among thousands of people all dressed up and with relaxed and pleasant expressions on their faces. It was as if I had crossed the border into another country.

However, to my eyes at least, they seemed to walk around without any clear direction and they did not seem to be waiting for anything in particular. I fell in with the crowd and just let my feet follow theirs. There seemed to be a certain rhythm and direction to the flow and I soon found myself on the pavement just across the street from the National Museum. I took up my position and waited. I did not know what I was waiting for, or even if there really was anything to wait for. However, having grown up in Norway, I had a clear picture of what a national day's celebration should look like: to me, the school children's parade in Oslo was a most powerful icon. So perhaps I was waiting for the parade.

But there was no parade. I stood on the pavement, like everyone else, enjoying the sun and watching people just standing or slowly walking along the street and there was probably nothing in my appearance that made me different from anyone else. But an anxiety started to arise in me, a fear that at any moment someone would step forward, address me and claim that, as a foreigner, I had no right to take part in *their* celebration. In order to mitigate the sense of estrangement or at least to indicate my presence as being friendly, I bought a green, white and red cockade and attached it to my lapel. Thus, by discretely disguising my foreign body and masquerading as a local, I tried to become as invisible as possible.

Of course, no one addressed me. But my anxiety made me aware of my inability to read the surroundings, both linguistically and with regard to its general cultural meaning. But at the same time I realised that this did not really matter in relation to my fellow celebrators: to them I was just a body among all the others – as they were to me. And as a body it was movements and actions that counted, not thoughts and ideas.

For a while nothing much happened, but gradually the crowd grew tighter in the small park at the foot of the steps leading to the museum. Maybe something was happening after all? I crossed the street and found my way into the park. Here people were obviously waiting for something. They paid attention to every unfamiliar sound and kept glancing at the small stage at the top of the steps, manoeuvring themselves to find a good vantage point. One movement led to another so that we all seemed to take part in a strange dance – without any obvious choreography but with a discernable pattern. My participation in this dance was also a way of being transplanted into the event by the way it became incorporated into my own body's movements (cp. Merleau-Ponty 1999:143).

However, mentally, I was still a stranger waiting for the school children's parade, so that although my body was present in this real-time-event – adjusting itself on impulse to try to find a good position with a view of the stage, and mimicking the movements of others in the crowd – my mind was somewhere else, preoccupied with national identity. I could sense an estrangement and felt that I was waiting for the materialisation of my own specific childhood memories. To put this in more general terms, one could say that my perceptual world did not match that of my reflections, and vice versa.

In order to be able to reflectively understand what was happening during this sunny day in Budapest, I had to try to get rid of my pre-conceptions. The idea of a 'perceptual approach' to fieldwork is to try to experience the actual constitution of the event in which one participates. Now, in the ordinary activities of everyday life, we are guided by past experiences (cp. Schutz 1967:79; Merleau-Ponty 1999:140). Our past experiences are present as an awareness of what to expect and do, a kind of confirmation that the world is ordered and meaningful. We usually know what to expect, such as which route the local bus will follow so that we are able to react if one day it takes an unexpected turn. In everyday life we develop what Schutz (1970:72f) calls a natural attitude. This is a central part of the lifeworld in which things and actions are taken for granted. It is also a world that we can operate within in order to confirm or change it, since we know how it works.

But in Budapest my natural attitude did not work. This became even more apparent when things started to happen at the top of the museum steps. The flags fluttered, some men started to play the kettledrums and women, in some kind of national dress that directed my thoughts to one of Wagner's operas, stepped forward and began to sing something that sounded serious. They were succeeded by speakers in neat suits. At the foot of the National museum steps, the atmosphere became rather listless. The speeches were numerous and long-winded. The applause more dutiful than enthusiastic. Actually, nothing much happened in terms of outward activities. But a sense of solemn festivity was present, even in a person like myself, who did not understand a word of what was being said. The place itself, the vague yet determined meaning materialised in the building's columnar facade, the wide, imposing steps and the little park between the building and the busy main street was in no way an accidentally chosen arena.[4] Without the monumental illusions in front of one's eyes, the staged event would not be more than a mere abstraction (cp. Augé 1995:60). The material culture was an essential part of the event.

Imaginative Empathy

Fieldwork-wise, I believe this was a crucial moment. Since I was not in command of the language, other impressions flooded over me. The strange language forced me to navigate the atmosphere with a greater sensitivity. It was my body rather than my mind that tied me to this world, and it seemed to come out of the surrounding space (cp. Merleau-Ponty 1999:148).

But my mind still worked flat out, testing perceptions in relation to previous experiences. I found myself trying to develop a kind of *imaginative empathy*, giving attention to the reactions of the people around me, and actively trying to put my own sentiments into the same gear as I imagined theirs were. I was trying to understand the others, that is, to experience *their* harmony between what they aimed at and what was given, between the intention and the performance (cp. Merleau-Ponty 1999:144). And I was doing this by using the sensations that arose from my bodily presence in the crowd. What was actually happening was that what was self-evident in my ordinary world was being challenged by this new one. It became apparent to me that through the bodily experience, several ways of being or living could find their way into the cultural instruments of celebrating belonging (cp. Merleau-Ponty 1999:348).

I was struggling with the motives as well as the meanings of the actions I observed.[5] As an observer I could only guess the meaning of the actions and the motives of the actors, judging from what I could see. Normally, in my everyday surroundings, I could be quite certain that my interpretation would correspond with the actors' ideas, but now I felt I could not be so sure.

Like the others, I enjoyed the warm spring sunshine, but unlike them I was a loner in the crowd. Most people did not seem to pay very much attention to what was going on at the top of the steps, but chatted with their families and friends. Judging from similar events in Scandinavia, where I do understand the language and can take in what is being said, I guessed that people were partly commenting on the event itself, but were mostly talking about other matters. This attitude – not feeling obliged to concentrate on what was taking place on stage – was significant in the celebration as a social event, but methodologically speaking, it posed a problem. In my case, being alone in a crowd made up of small groups, I had great difficulty in using imaginative empathy. Their small talk underlined my position as an outsider.[6] I tried to think myself into similar situations in which I had really participated, and use those recollections to imagine what was going on in the present crowd.

Thus I was trying to break out of the limitations set by my own vision. What I wanted to do was to '… break the link between my vision and the world, between myself and my vision, in order to catch and describe it' (Merleau-Ponty 1999:227).

My body was the instrument used to pick up the event, but in order to understand its meaning, I had to reflect upon the perceptions. This reflection would naturally have been much simpler if I had had a native to discuss it with. Since I did not have that, I instead started to have an imagined conversation with myself. In concrete terms I was walking, standing, looking, listening, smelling, sensing, and at the same time telling myself stories, testing which story would make the most sense, carry the highest credibility as a reflection on my experiences, and at the same time, posing the questions I wanted to find answers to. In this way, I actively turned my attention to the event in order to find its meaning (cp. Schutz 1967:71).

I later found out that the celebration at the National Museum had been officially arranged by the Government.. The political implications of that did not occur to me during the event, but I started to suspect it when, at the end of the speeches, I accompanied the stream of people through the streets. In what seemed to me as an outsider to be the commercial centre, we encountered a demonstration. I could not really understand what was actually going on here either; who was demonstrating or why, and how it was related to the celebration of the nation. In contrast to the activity by the steps of the National Museum, the atmosphere around the demonstration was highly charged. The demonstrators expressed their anger and their dissatisfaction by chants, placards and banners, and the aggressive body language of the marchers spread to the bystanders. I imagined that someone had tried to (politically) 'steal' the nation, although whether this someone came from the political left or the right I could not judge. In contrast to the government's celebration, the demonstration was not tied to a specific place. It moved through the centre in such a way – through its very movement – as to symbolically seize the town. At the same time it became much more ephemeral. As soon as the demonstration had passed, it was as though it had never taken place. Only the sound of it still echoed after the marchers had disappeared from sight.

Walking along with the crowd, I had the very strong feeling that I was an unqualified actor – I could not even work out whether the demonstrators were right or left wing. The problem was that I could not really understand the others' action as a carrier or indicator of their intended meaning. I was trying to use my own lived experience as a guide, but projecting my own experiences of Scandinavian political demonstrations really made no sense (cp. Schutz 1967:107ff).

I thought I had understood the demonstration, since it matched some of my previous experiences. But the events at the foot of the museum steps did not match any of my previous experiences. Because of that, I could not interpret its meaning. If I hadn't been told that this was the celebration of Hungary's national day, I would never have guessed. But I would have been able to say that this was some kind of celebration, by reading the postures and actions of people around me, and also the staged event itself. So one could say that material culture and the bodily activities of people help us understand the atmosphere of events, but not necessarily their meaning and intention. For this we need language.

Understanding Meanings

Being qualified as an actor is about knowing what general meanings are attached to different kinds of phenomena in a specific society. In the things we take for granted, this knowledge cannot really be said to be normative in any practical sense. For example, political knowledge consists of our ability to tell the difference between right and left, thus enabling us to take a political stand. It does not, however, mean that we can dictate it. The general knowledge of a society is not external to the actions of everyday life, but rather inherent in them, as structures and conditions and as the actors' own plans and ambitions (Hansen 1998:184ff). In such processes, images of belonging are important points of reference.

Actions[7] are always exercised according to a preconceived plan in which what one does in the present is projected into the future. Any action will, however, be characterized by the past, since the planning takes place before the action has been performed. My previous experience guided my initial attempts to understand what I encountered in Budapest, and made me choose between the Norwegian and the Swedish national holidays – of which I have personal knowledge – as the guiding experience in understanding what was going on. Since the Swedish national holiday is hardly ever celebrated, it was natural that I should use the recollections of my Norwegian childhood as a guideline. But when this quickly proved to be of little help in understanding the event, I had to develop a new, improvised plan by reorganizing the structure of my recollection of past experiences in relation to what was happening now.

When discussing intersubjective understanding, Schutz outlines two ideal situations. The first occurs when the actor merely seeks to bring about changes in the external world. The second one occurs when the actor seeks to consciously communicate his/her mind to others (Schutz 1967:113ff). But what I was dealing with, not only in Budapest, but in the other fields that I encountered, were situations that were created – or staged – in order to trigger off sentiments of a more or less specific kind. My purpose was not to investigate the motives of the creators of the events, but to understand what was taking place when people acted in them. What I was dealing with was a complex arrangement of signs, or symbols, into which people were walking and acting. To most of the actors, there was probably a shared fundamental meaning of the totality of signs, i.e. 'we are here to celebrate our nation, Hungary'. This was quite apparent, even to a total outsider like myself. But on the level of the individual actors, we are apt to find several different ways of linking the perceptual arrangement of signs to the stock of experiences with its recollections of the past and strategies for the future.

New experiences are thus weighed in relation to old ones and already established meanings are modified. We constantly change the meanings that condition the activities we participate in (Nilsén 2000: 44). If 'culture' is seen as having something to do with making and understanding meanings, then this example shows how it develops from a constant testing and questioning of shared experiences, of shared relations and everyday lives. 'Culture' therefore cannot be seen as something static or as a 'steady category' (Stewart 1996:40). Rather 'culture' should be seen as an expectation, a way to plan and understand the actions of oneself and others in the world, a never-ending pursuit of something that is constantly changing. This is a way of approaching the field that differs from the prevailing modernist theories, which tend to see people in their relationship to the world as being totally steered by their intellects, and thus capable of narrating this to an inquisitive fieldworker. The risk in following such an analytical track is that people's actions are read as *reactions*, so that consciousness and intellectual dimensions are overemphasized. As a result, expectations, bodily experiences and activities tend to stay in the background. In contrast to thinking, reflecting and ideologies, the sensual, physical and material experiences are hidden.[8]

Turning our focus from compensatory escapes to experiencing the life world, from modernist (or post-modernist) to phenomenological perspectives, puts a new stress on the way we do fieldwork. What is needed is a shift from participant *observation* to shared *experience*, from what people *say* to what they *do*. Being there – taking part in the activities and events we want to study – is a way of changing our focus from words to deeds, and letting people be responsible for their own actions.

One of the main methodological arguments for trying to conduct fieldwork through participant experience is to move it away from the heavy reliance on words, which has characterized most of modern ethnological work – and still continues to do so. Possibly this dominance of words, spoken as well as written, is not only a result of how we, the academic intellectuals, tend to see the world, but also something which might be traced back to the enlightenment's strong beliefs in rational thinking. But life, of course, is made up of so much more than words and rational decisions, and our experience of the world is not primarily narrative, but rather sensory. Just talking about hunger, pain, happiness or love is not the same thing as experiencing them. It might, therefore, be worthwhile to try to develop methods for reaching those first-hand experiences, rather than relying on hearing stories about them. And, naturally, this also goes for the kind of sentiments being triggered off by celebrations of belonging, no matter whether these are national, local, or familial.

I do know that no one can ever *be* another person. There are limits to both imagination and empathy. But there really is no need to exaggerate the differences between the researchers and those who inhabit the places in which we carry out our fieldwork. On the contrary, there is a lot to be said about the similarities between us.

Was It Worth It?

There are certain implications for those writing ethnographic texts based on this way of approaching the field. In their Writing Culture (1986), Clifford & Marcus have already begun to question the structure of ethnographic texts. Their critique may be summed up in the question about who has the right to interpret what takes place in the field. Even though I agree with much of their critique, I do not agree with their solution. On the contrary, I believe that as researchers, we must be willing to take full responsibility for the texts we produce – even when we let the voices of 'the natives' be heard. First of all, the fieldworker must be visible, since his/her sensory impressions are the starting point for the analysis. The fieldworker must therefore be an ever-present ego in the text, as must the concreteness of the surroundings. The senses that arise within are always unequivocally connected to the place in which they arise. Transparency enables the reader to reflect on his/her own experiences, and thus to evaluate and take up a position in relation to what is being presented. Transparency, then, is necessary even when the text turns from personal, sensory impressions and changes to a more general argument. On the other hand, the use of one's own perceptions as a source will change the standards for referring to the empirical material. By that I mean we will move from a 'positivist' focus on strict documentation, to a narrative that relies on its own trustworthiness. In turn, this will only be possible if the researcher is able to generalize his or her personal experiences in a way that is meaningful to the reader. A perception cannot be repeated in a scientific sense, but it can be presented so that the reader recollects perceptions of his or her own.

But turning fieldwork into a text is also a way of bringing order to a chaotic and disorganized real life. One might even say that meeting this world through fieldwork is meeting it with a gaze that is an ordering, plot-creating gaze. And, as I have related earlier in this text, I have even used the plot-centered technique of actively telling myself stories in order to try to understand my field. This, however, is also what characterizes scientific writing and differentiates it from fiction. What we are finally aiming at is trying to understand the actors' motives. But this is in reality a different task, and the researcher will, according to Schutz, have to be satisfied with three indirect approaches:

> 1. He can search his memory for similar actions of his own, and finding such, can draw from them a general principle concerning the relation of their in-order-to and because-motives. …
> 2. Lacking such a guideline, he can resort to his own knowledge of the customary behavior of the person observed and from this deduce the latter's in-order-to and because-motives. …
> 3. … His last resort will then be to try to infer the in-order-to motive from the act by asking whether such and such a motive would be furthered by the act in question [Schutz 1967:174f].

All these approaches imply inserting order in the world.

There are resemblances between the method sketched out here, and what is usually called participant observation. The main difference is that I have been trying to work from the fact that I was a stranger in the situation, and that my participation was that of an outsider trying to imagine what it would be like to be an insider.

A new kind of fieldwork needs to concentrate on the processes involved when places are made to represent culture and identity. This is what is meant when we say that we need to concentrate on how places are made to happen. Or as the American philosopher Edward Casey has put it: 'A place is more an event than a thing to be assimilated to known categories'(Casey 1996:26).

A Fieldwork of Perceptions?

The most striking feeling I had both during and after this fieldwork-session[9] was a sense of non-belonging. In writing the original text, I felt I was balancing on the edge of literature. On the other hand, putting myself actively and consciously in the position of the outsider certainly enhanced my sensitivity towards the activity of doing fieldwork.

Analytically speaking, ethnography is not pure description but rather an ongoing process of explanation and interpretation, since we, as researchers, are usually part of the same universe of meanings as the people we study. The understanding we have of what is going on in 'the field' is not only developed by what is actually taking place there, but also by the inferences we make using knowledge gained from outside the field. The experiment that I carried out helped me to understand more about the way these inferences work. They will usually normalise any situation we enter, since we habitually try to find a parallel in our previous experience. Analytically, it is therefore important to be conscious of the sensory impulses that actually start off the process.

The example used in this article turns our attention to the importance of language as a means of understanding the world, but also in becoming a real part of any world. Language is a way of picking up the thoughts of others, and a way of trying to think as they do. I could not do this and was therefore unable to get any notion of all the tailored meanings inherent in speech. Turning oneself into an outsider means placing oneself outside the thoughts that are present in language, as objects ready to be used by actors (cp. Merleau-Ponty 1999:179).

One might argue[10] that this kind of fieldwork, and especially placing oneself outside language, makes it difficult or impossible to understand and grasp such phenomena as intentionality, agency, social relations, local knowledge and lifeworlds. These are all tightly integrated with language, and need real, not imaginative, empathy. On the other hand, the experiment in fieldwork described here turned out to give several insights and a more profound sensitivity towards material culture, landscape, settings, and place.

Of course we might gain some insights into everyday life, in the sense of unreflected, lived reality, dominated by 'the natural attitude' (Schutz, 1970:72f). Successful fieldwork should be characterized by reaching into this natural, unreflected attitude towards reality. Thus it means losing oneself as a reflecting intellectual – not forever, but as a methodological move, in order to establish the imaginative empathy that will bring us closer to perceiving events and places in the same manner as the locals. So, in walking around Budapest, I was trying to catch something; something that I could claim would most resemble the feelings the locals seemed to have towards the celebrations.[11]

It might seem difficult to find a way into the natural attitudes of other people, but it is even harder to try to grasp the ways in which they create meaning of their perceptions. This process might be described as the way perceptions are turned into lived experience. And previous experiences do influence those of the present, without really being problematised by the individual. Acting in the world takes place against a background of preconditions that we take for granted – and previous experiences are an integral part of these preconditions.

As acting individuals we have experiences which we carry with us through life. Social life is dependent on the individual's capability to make sense of and understand meaning, and previous experience plays an important role in this. But when we state that meaning is the exact significance the actor puts into the action, then it becomes clear that knowledge of meaning belongs to the actor, and not to the observer. 'Thought is focused on the object of the spatiotemporal world; life pertains to duration. The tension between the two is of the essence of the "meaningfulness" of experience. It is misleading to say that experiences have meaning. Meaning does not lie in the experience. Rather, those experiences are meaningful which are grasped reflectively. The meaning is the way in which the Ego regards its experience.' (Schutz 1967:69)

In addition, meaning/significance is not given once and for all. It is created and recreated through actions and reflections – and is very often dependent on the actual situation which brought it to the fore. To reach beyond this, it is necessary to focus upon the lived experience, that is on the pre-reflective experience of perception.

One of the purposes of the fieldwork-experiment was to problematise the background of taken-for-granted conditions by challenging my own. By taking the perceiving, experiencing, and acting subjective individual – that is myself – as a starting point, I tried to make the pre-reflective perceptions more visible, and thus the whole process of fieldwork more transparent. Such first-order experiences are truly bound to me as a subject, but they can then be used in order to understand the experiences of others. In the experiment I did not accomplish this, but the idea was to use the personal experience of the fieldworker as a starting point for dialogues with other actors in the same situation, and thus to create a better understanding of the process through which meanings are attached to events. 'Applied to the theory of behavior, this means that one's own behavior, while it is actually taking place, is a *prephenomenal* experience. Only when it has already taken place ... does it stand out as a discrete item from the background of one's other experiences. Phenomenal experience is therefore never of oneself behaving, only of having behaved. Yet the original experience in another sense remains the same in memory as it was when it occurred.' (Schutz 1967:56)

Fieldwork-wise this causes a problem. As a stranger – and as a professional fieldworker – it would be highly unlikely that my experiences coincided with those of the locals acting in the same situation. It became obvious in the interpretations I made in order to make sense and meaning of my perceptions of the Hungarian national celebration that I could not abstain from using my own experiences, or my academic knowledge. In the process of making sense of perceptions, I left the realm of imaginative empathy and re-entered my own realm of European ethnology. Working in this manner is obviously open to highly subjective interpretations. On the other hand, the acts and events that I dealt with were such that anyone could compare them with their own experiences and interpretations. The reader might choose to reject or accept them – to be a stranger to or to recognize himself/herself in the situations and interpretations that I have presented here.

Notes

1 Social anthropologists have criticised how we, the ethnologists, perform our fieldwork, but I will not go into this here.
2 Although oversimplified, this is the description given in a much-used Swedish textbook entitled 'Field Ethnology' (Arnstberg 1997).
3 It should be noted that this article is written in the aftermath of the real event

not only regarding the time span, but inevitably also in relation to new reflections having been made.

4   The National Museum is exactly what the name indicates: a kind of essence of the nation where Hungary distinctly stands out as the final outcome of a historic development. In the exhibitions inside the museum, the nation begins with the arrival of the Magyars to the high tableland and concludes with the fall of Communism. Throughout, all the difficulties and distress of the nation have been brought to light.

5   According to Schutz (1967:30) a motive is the expectations that an actor has on his action, while meaning refers to the significance the action has for the actor. Of course, this is a knowledge that resides with the actor, not the observer.

6   One solution would be to have gone there with friends, but this would have diminished my concentration on what actually took place at the event.

7   Schutz makes a distinction between behaviour, which in the lived experience will only have meaning through reflection and thereby only when it has already been done (Schutz 1967:55f), and action, which is always performed according to a plan that is projected on to the future. Actions will therefore necessarily have a character of the past, since their meanings are built from previous experiences that are projected into the future (Schutz 1967:57ff).

8   There are important political dimensions to this. Policies construct subjects as objects of power. They are tools, which, in the Foucauldian tradition, could be analyzed as the translation of political interests into common knowledge. Another aspect of this could be termed re-subjectification: the way that policies are met not only through adaptation or resistance, but also with completely new ways of acting and new cultural forms. This should lead us to question ideas that idealize the homogenizing effects of policy-decisions and underline that the objects of these decisions are not objects in any true sense. People are active and acting subjects, following their own goals and ambitions. On the other hand, they usually have less power than the policy makers concerning the possibilities of carrying through their visions.

9   The session included all the different fieldworks used in the article mentioned earlier.

10   I am grateful to Prof. Jonas Frykman for suggesting these points.

11   This might sound like a romantic idea about going instantly native. The point however is that when this is realised as a conscious act of reflection, there is also a conscious distance between oneself and the natives.

References

Arnstberg, Karl-Olov 1997: *Fältetnologi.* Stockholm: Carlssons.

Augé, Marc 1995: *Non-places. Introduction to an Anthropology of Supermodernity.* London: Verso.

Casey Edward 1998: *The Fate of Place. A Philosophical History.* Berkely: University of California Press.

Clifford, James & Marcus, George E. 1986 (eds): *Writing Culture. The Poetics and Politics of Ethnography.* Berkeley: University of California Press.

Ehn, Billy (red.) 1993: *Kultur och erfarenhet. Aktuella teman i svensk etnologi.* Stockholm: Carlssons.

Gupta, Akhil & Ferguson, James 1992: Beyond 'Culture': Space, Identity, and the Politics of Difference. *Cultural Anthropology*, 7 (1).

Gupta, Akhil & Ferguson, James 1997: Discipline and Practice: 'The Field' as Site, Method, and Location in Anthropology. In Gupta & Ferguson (eds): *Anthropological Locations. Boundaries and Grounds of a field science.* Berkeley: University of California Press.

Hansen, Kjell 1998: *Välfärdens motsträviga utkant.* Lund: Historiska Media.

Hansen, Kjell 2001: Just Behind the Next Corner – Doing Fieldwork on the Europe of Everyday Life. I: Ewy Rewers & Jacka Sójki (eds): *Man Within Culture at the Threshold of the 21st Century.* Poznan: Wydawnictwo Fundacji humaniora.

Hansen, Kjell 2003: Festivals, Spatiality, and the New Europe. *Ethnologia Europaea* 32:2.

Merleau-Ponty, Maurice 1999 (1962): *Phenomenology of Perception.* London & New York: Routledge.

Nilsén, Åke 2000: 'En empirisk vetenskap om duet'. *Om Alfred Schutz bidrag till sociologin.* Lund: Lund Dissertations in Sociology 34.

Schutz, Alfred 1967: *The Phenomenology of the Social World.* Northwestern University Studies in Phenomenology & Existential Philosophy. Evanston, Illinois: Northwestern University Press.

Schutz, Alfred 1970: *On Phenomenology and Social relations.* Edited and with an Introduction by Helmut R. Wagner. Chicago and London: The University of Chicago Press.

Stewart, Kathleen 1996: *A Space on the Side of the Road. Cultural Poetics in an 'Other' America.* Princeton: Princeton University Press.

JONAS FRYKMAN

Between History and Material Culture

On European Regionalism and the Potentials of Poetic Analysis

> Space that has been seized upon by the imagination cannot re-main indifferent space subject to the measures and estimate by the surveyor. It has been lived in, not in its positivity, but with all the partiality of the imagination.
>
> Gaston Bachelard, 1964/1994:xxxvi

A decade ago, the common European conference of SIEF (Société Internationale d'Ethnologie et de Folklore) met in Bergen, Norway. It was then dealing with the topic of Modernity and how ethnology was trying to embrace new perspectives on national issues. This year SIEF met in Budapest, Hungary and the theme was 'Times, Places, Passages'. Never before has there been such an abundance of papers containing the single word 'Europe'. Together with 'locality' and 'belonging' words like 'memory, identity, heritage, region and nation' kept appearing in plenary lectures and thematic sessions. What we have been witnessing during the last few years is a slow turn from Ethnology *in* the different *countries* of Europe – to the Ethnology *of Europe* in different countries. European Ethnology is taking such an active part in the grand narrative of Europe that it is worth while discussing what the particular contribution of our discipline will be. Is it yet another contribution to the well-known success-story of European civilisation: 'From Plato to Nato' (cf. Shore 2000, Frykman 2001) – the grand narrative that portrays the continent in the light of its great spirits, its elite culture. Or will it disclose how an everyday europeanisation *from below* is taking place? Over the ages Europe has seen massive waves of migration, an intense transportation of goods and material culture – and not only by lorries on the highways – together with a wide exchange of attitudes and ideas. The numerous borders that have been and today are defining a European habitus have also been intense zones of contact over the centuries. For the majority of its inhabitants, Europe has not so much been an idea or a history of belonging, as a practice of travels, contacts and change.

Today, the mere notion of belonging seems to be one of the most problematic issues to be dealt with in contemporary European research. It implies a rootedness to place – a cultural identity that makes territory, the home-place or 'Heimat' its very foundation (Morley & Robins 1995). Certainly more mobile identifications could be envisaged such as class, gender, occupation or ethnicity. The notion of belonging seems to hold a *contradictio in adjecto* – opposing the very idea of europeanisation from below as meaning contacts over borders and practices of change – by denoting that people have to stay put in order to be truly European. Today we can follow how a rapid formation of cultural identities is taking place in many nations and even more regions. To be recognised as a true European citizen or minority, a distinct culture or society must identify people – they must have a territory. This is more obvious within the EU, where ethnic minorities within countries are recognised – with a few exceptions like the Romes, Sami or Jews – solely on a territorial basis. The tools for this cultural construction of rooted cultural identities are mostly found in the archives and museums founded by ethnologists in the 19th and 20th Centuries (Klein 1996). Through a cultural heritage drawn from the most static of popular cultures – the peasantry – a virtual dream-world is constructed, a world that meets the demands of the present. In European nations and regions, belonging therefore assumes the face of a general cultural critique. Contemporary images of globalisation, technologisation and exploitation are being challenged. Rootedness has become an alternative, the Other, held up as a remedy for today's shortcomings (Stewart 1996). Early ethnology can draw on an abundance of information to support this challenge. *Volkskunde* was founded as a nostalgic commentary on the modernisation of 19th Century rural life. Rallying behind local, regional or national values and cultural identities is supported by right wing political parties. A wide range of populist and reactionary political movements thrive whenever the genuine, authentic and domestic is used as a contrast to threatening invasions from abroad. But the issue is much more complex, since identification with place and territory seems to be one of the most prominent sources of cultural identity in the Europe of today.

The dilemma that ethnologists are caught up in is on the one hand to promote the importance of appreciating popular culture and on the other hand to take a stand against the use or abuse of the image of a popular culture constructed using information provided by their predecessors. This often results in them showing how regional identification is a phenomenon close to false consciousness and they too easily end up in the trap of illustrating how any regional or national identity fits together in bits and pieces. As will be discussed at length, I think that this deconstructive turn in ethnology is close to missing a profound insight as to why place and belonging have become important. It seems as if belonging to place has been taken as a matter of ideology by ethnologists rather than of practice, as if being judged by what it stands for instead of what it is used for. And the use could be a wide range of practices – from xenophobic denunciation of anyone who is different from us, to seeing the region as an arena where cultural encounters are taking place and where the surrounding world is being mediated in a recognisable form. Above all it is like a branding of something that is reliable, recognisable and authentic. For example, food that is labelled with its precise geographical origin is to be trusted (Salomonsson 2001). However, in venturing on such a path of analysis, ethnologists seem to be forced to turn their attention away from ideas, history and cultural constructs towards action, material objects and practice. The question that remains is not what a region *is*, but how it *happens*. That implies taking both the landscape and material culture seriously, to try to discover the intention and consequences of people's actions and paying less attention to how agency is motivated.

I will be using the region of Istria in Croatia to analyse how history and memory – as well as acknowledged cultural heritage – are being interpreted, particularly with regard to the poetic dimension. In order to illustrate what I mean by the poetic dimension, I will focus on the culturally generative, showing how things happen rather than what they are. I will draw on the findings of a comparative European research-project where regions and places in Norway, Sweden, Germany, Austria, Croatia, Slovenia and Poland have come under scrutiny.[1] Later on, I will return to the question of how Istria started to 'happen' in the 90's. But I want to start with a description of a meeting in the town of Pula that I found puzzling, then discuss the hesitancy that ethnologists have towards place and belonging and conclude with further references to Istria.

'They Breathe This Air'

On a clear February afternoon in 1999, I was sitting in a badly heated room on the second floor of the Faculty of Pedagogics at Pula University. The white building with its classicist architecture, situated on a hill and overlooking this old town, used to be an Italian training college for schoolteachers. After taking their exams, the new teachers were expected to spread the language and culture in multilingual Istria. I was there to talk to Professor Nelida Milani Kruljac. Having the rare position of being an intellectual and an influential member and co-founder of the regional party – IDS (Istrian Democratic Association) – she was the ideal person with whom to discuss multiculturalism and cultural heritage in Istria. IDS is just one of the many new parties in Europe that is using local issues as a political platform.

Professor Milani teaches Italian at university level. Born into an Italian speaking family, she is married to a Croat and speaks Croatian at home. Her own life reflects the rather striking pluralism of the whole region. There are three major linguistic groups – Croats, Slovenes and Italians. In addition, Macedonian, Albanian, Serbian, and Ruthene are spoken in the area. At the previous *fin de siecle,* Austrian ethnologists regarded Istria as the Utopia of a pre-national culture where people of many different origins were living together without being divided by artificial borders (Kappus 2001).

There is nothing strange about a region that harbours so many ethnic groups, although it might sound confusing from a homogenous Scandinavian perspective. What has made Istria a gratifying field of study – for me and for a growing number of ethnologists and anthropologists – is the fact that it is letting the many ethnic groups contribute to the development of a firm foundation of a territorial, regional identity. This has not been the experience of many of the countries that emerged out of a dissolving Yugoslavia, where ethnic cleansing seemed to be a preferred way of dealing with multiethnicity. Since 1995 IDS has successfully promoted the idea of Istria as a Euro-region, thereby setting an example for Croatia, the country to which most of the peninsula belongs.

The regional party, IDS, considers Istria to be a role model for Europe. Istria seems to be that rare place where it is possible, in the words of Milan Rakovac, the former editor of the regional newspaper, *Glas Istre*, to: 'recognise a pluralism that is letting languages, cultures and ethnicities flourish. And if this is possible in Istria, it would be possible also elsewhere' (1996, 2001). Is this perhaps that much sought-after place where the nation-state is being superseded in the local, where state-power is being de-territorialised and then re-territorialised in forms that are more adapted to a globalised world (Appadurai 1996)?

Whenever multiculturalism and tolerance are raised on the political agenda, you should beware of empty rhetoric. At most territorial levels today, xenophobia is growing. The regionalisation of Europe implies that regions are looked upon as if they were more natural spaces – while the entire *EU-rope* and to some extent the nation states are held to be spurious. As a region is always rooted in its proper place it opens up to a rhetoric that by using cultural heritage, 'memory, loss, and nostalgia plays directly into the hands of reactionary popular movements' (Gupta & Ferguson 1992:13). There is hardly a country in Europe where a Jean-Marie Le Pen, Jörg Haider, Christoph Blocher, Umberto Bossi, Carl I Hagen or Pia Kjaersgaard are not using the language of *Heimat* to produce an image of cultural identity that has more or less grown organically from place. In the conversations with professor Nelida Milani Kruljac, the question to be answered was how a regional cultural identity could be bound up with multiculturalism without leading to homelessness.

'In the families people have been a practising multiculturalism over the generations,' she said. 'You have different faces depending on whom you are meeting. Is it friends, family, officials?' This had developed into a strategy because people were aware of the place remaining but the rulers were always shifting.

> By keeping to the variety you have been able to keep clear of the homogenising claims from afar. In the beginning of the century, Istria was ruled by the Habsburgs; after the First World War it was fascist Italy; after the next war it was socialist Yugoslavia and now it is the nation-states of Croatia and Slovenia. Since the 50's and onwards, people from many parts of former Yugoslavia intermarried. Istria was a true immigration-part of the Socialist Federation of Yugoslavia. People then acquired an everyday competence in dealing with the many backgrounds and different languages. But this had long roots in history. By sticking to the very local, people have been able to escape the demands from the centre – in whatever country this has been situated. 'Istrianity' became a constantly shifting image – also in the face of socialism where every ethnic group was expected to take the stage, performing their identity in folk-costumes, dances and folk music. Our *convivenza* – *suživot* (which denotes co-living or co-habitation) also could be understood as an answer to these shifting conditions.

'Paradoxically, identifying with Istria became a matter of *not* learning about its history,' she continued, 'since it is more the lack of a coherent narration that builds up our identity. Ours is not the history of Vienna, Rome, Belgrade, or Zagreb.' The master narratives have always been fought by local pluralism. There seemed to be a strong continuity in this everyday behaviour up to the present day.

In this interview, Nelida Milani Kruljac claimed the same for the Istrian population at large as the Slovene ethnologist Borut Brumen (2001) has argued for the villagers of the small border-village of Sveti Petar. Rather than regarding the past as history, they saw it as 'tradition', which made them alert to rewriting the story of their identity. How could they believe in history when every state had a different version of it? They had been living 'pod', *under* different regimes. Truth about the past – whether it was *under* the Austrians, the Fascists, the Yugoslavs or the Slovenes – had been adapted to suit the demands of the time. The only bridge between the past and the present was the place itself, with its nature and particular memories – its traditions. Historical time had therefore been overtaken by social time, merging people and place into one. 'If a community is forced into redefining its identities, then it can, as was the case of ... Sveti Petar, respond also with a reconceptualisation of tradition' (Brumen 2001:12).

Professor Milani Kruljac – a learned scholar and very experienced in local cultural issues – then added something which for a long time had me puzzled. Until then she had told me what I had expected to hear: the historical background of this multiculturalism and the cultural construction on which such an apparently strong regional identification must rest. Since we had both done our homework on how a national or regional identity is fitted together, we knew that any such identity is made up of the symbols, the land and its holy places, the language and the history.

It certainly was rewarding to hear how the influencial regional press – *Glas Istre* – The Voice of Istria – was keeping the region informed, how the ancient *cajkavian* dialect was supported by regional and local bodies and also to learn about the importance of the school system. In particular, the schooling was fascinating, taking into account the training college we were sitting in. During the fascist era, between the two World Wars, Croatian was banned in schools and only Italian was taught. The famous *convivenza* thus took on another meaning of subjugation, leading to poverty on Italian terms only. Living together under Yugoslav socialism after World War II meant that most languages were accepted as long as they had nothing to do with fascism and Italy! The majority of the population was by then Italian speaking. The interview was long and very informative – or at least it told me what I had been asking for. However, just before we parted, she said, *en passant* whilst looking out of the window: 'People who come here, breathe this air, go to these beaches, eat this food – so what can they become but Istrians?'

It was not until some time later, when I had become increasingly aware of the use of the many qualities existing in the landscape, that I understood the real significance of what she had been saying. It was neither mocking the cold February day, nor playing with the stereotype of the millions of tourists that appeared every summer, nor defying the importance of history and past experiences. On the contrary, she was underlining these factors, but also pointing to something so obvious that it was almost embarrassing not to have understood immediately: The lack of history in the sense of grand narrative made place emerge with an intensified significance.

A local cultural identity was 'made', not only constructed using local traditions and social life but also by the material potential of the landscape – sky, cliffs, water, medieval towns, cattle, food, wines – in short exploring the material culture for its potential to induce dreams and feed the imagination. It amounted to something much more than what David Lowenthal two decades ago coined as 'heritage' in contrast to 'history' (1985), thereby denoting that history is used for constructing something personally important out of the past, a legacy about a place-bound identity. Here I have been using the word *poetics* with a reference to Gaston Bachelard's ideas about fantasy, creativity and the human potential for constantly 'making the world new' (1969). Bachelard is persistently advocating the importance of getting rid of the intellectual habit of seeking the rationale of imagination. The poetic image, he says 'is essentially *variational*, and not, as in the case of the concept, constitutive'. Bringing in the image of the poem he states, that 'the reader of poems is asked to consider an image not as an object and even less as the substitute for an object, but to seize its specific reality' (1969:xix). In the present day discussion, *cultural heritage* usually represents a collection of stories and objects, but misses out how it is constantly reshaped and reorganised in new and meaningful forms. In stressing the poetic qualities, the dynamic and generative power of objects and stories are brought to the fore. Understanding the formation of this multicultural region turned out to be shifting attention away from what Istria *was* in some kind of nomothetic sense of the word, to how it *happened* in forms ever new and how it became filled with life and meaning in the everyday.

In 1992, the then vice-president of Istria, Loredana Debeljuh, wrote about the importance of this very landscape as an identity-formation that could hold the different ethnicities together. Istria, she said, was offering a peculiar form of authenticity, of knowing oneself and by the same token getting to know the landscape. Both self and landscape feasted on the existence of riddles and secrets. 'I am firmly convinced, and I deduce it intuitively, that in the heart of hearts – which has remained authentic – Istria continues to keep its secrets in that intimate language each of us know how to establish with the landscapes we love, because this is part of human nature our need for rootedness. Istria has this peculiar kind of authenticity, which is Slavic and Italian.' (Quoted from Ballinger 1999:14).

The American anthropologist Pamela Ballinger, who has been writing extensively on the history of Istrian regionalism, concluded that in Debeljuh's formulation, it was precisely the historical and authentic character of this multi-ethnicity, which then provided the basis for a regionalist movement. I was ready to say the same, if my interpretations had not been challenged by that mystifying statement about 'breathing this air'. History seems to have paved the way for a more intense attention to place and to landscape. What was there to be sensed and seen by Istrians and locals alike was available to everyone – including the visitor. The poetic imagination, which I suppose both Dr Debeljuh and Dr Milani Kruljac were talking about, is not necessarily divided according to ethnic belonging or knowledge about local history.

If this is so, then the researcher must put more emphasis on how people's actions, experiences and dreams have become conditioned by the place-bound and material. The methodological consequences could be that the many new regional identities in today's Europe must also be analysed by close reading and by using the observation and imagination of the researcher – the observation of something that is difficult to explain because it is always there. Unlike the social structure, the economy, narration and history, it can hardly be grasped from the armchair. As water is to fish, the material surrounding is so obvious that it becomes invisible. People always are, to use a Heideggerian term, 'embedded in the world' – meaning that they do not first of all ponder the material world, but tend to 'think and act *through* material objects.' Consciousness is by no means free-floating but always 'consciousness of *something*' (Crang 1998:109). This demands fieldwork, empirical studies *in situ*. What are people doing? How are they using the territory, material culture and heritage? How are these dimensions present in their actions without even having to be articulated? Added to this must surely be the constant but pleasant training of the fieldworkers' own poetic imagination.

I will come back to the case of poetic analysis, but first let me take you on a short tour of some of the more problematic areas concerning place and cultural heritage as foundations for identity-constructions in Europe today.

EU-Identities

Last year, together with some ten colleagues, I sent in an application to the Fifth Frame Programme 'Improving the socio-economic knowledge basis' within the European Commission. The goal of this effort in European co-operation was, and still is, to finance a study of how regions have become culturally colonised in different countries. In this comparative study project we wanted to find out how different regions *happen*. How are landscapes and artefacts used in the creation of something new; of dreams and possibilities that are offered the certainty of the physical place but not the demands of already given definitions? But also making a critical scrutiny into how many regions long for a homogeneous and well-controlled world where the boundaries between them and us are sharp and difficult to cross. In parallel to such openness, the much-discussed micro-nationalism is also growing.

The background for our proposal was political, since we wanted to produce deeper field-insights into the well-known threat coming from neo-nationalism in the nation-states and provincialism or micro-nationalism in the regions and places we were scrutinising. We took the position that, by working with popular culture – or *Volkskultur* – European ethnology had a unique opportunity to provide the insider's view. We could rely on the history of the discipline and at the same time give support to the importance of observing the ways and lives of people in the everyday. By looking at different European countries we could also make clarifying contrasts. In the Scandinavian countries, the 19th-century *Volkskultur* was made into a political icon and used for creating a democratic, common ground. In Norway the belief in a free and independent 19th-century peasantry became the main symbol for national autonomy – a large part of the population takes to the streets in folk-costumes on May 17th. In other countries such symbols also stand for exclusivity and self-sufficiency.

The very same *Volkskultur* has become one of the main excuses for keeping hold of what is ours, warding off immigrants and expelling refugees. But is it only ideas about moral superiority based upon cultural heritage that are at stake here? Is it only a re-action, a conviction that our past should be preserved in the face of an advancing dissolution? Is it really true that people prefer living in stable societies that can endure almost everything except change? It is true that in most of the peaceful and egalitarian Scandinavian countries xenophobia is rising – to say nothing about Austria, Belgium, Spain and France …? But is that really due to the fact that territory, region or nation is becoming the main source of identification? It is true that a *new* territoriality and use of *Volkskultur* seems to be rearing its head. This movement is no longer a process from *above* as in the times of fascism – as in the 1930's – but has become a growing popular concern.

These were the questions we wanted to bring to the fore. A study where we wanted to examine not so much what this obsession with heritage and place *was* as how it was *used* for different purposes in different countries and regions. Perhaps we were inventive in proposing a comparison of a wide range of more or less mobile cultural artefacts. How were new identities formulated in the various fields of regional food, theme parks with historical motifs and in historical dramas depicting local history? How do the local fairs and markets that are flourishing all over Europe define places and how has the physical landscape been re-enchanted and filled with importance in poetry and 'New Age'?[2]

We were not successful in getting the project funded. We did get a very illuminating answer from Brussels, however. Our elaborate ideas were reduced to a pragmatic essence by people used to looking at applications from the perspective of social and economical sciences: 'The project does refer to EU policies regarding cultural and identity issues by examining the way traditional culture is presented in different European settings ... By examining the way traditional culture is preserved in different European settings it can help new EU policies on cultural issues.'

It might be that we were using a vocabulary that was too vague because what was understood from Brussels was that this project fitted well into the much approved politics of strengthening local identities by means of history and cultural heritage! The answer also gave an interesting demonstration of how a European ethnology was being identified with the protection of any rural pattern from the last century – or regional variation in peasant culture.

European Ethnology

A special interpretation of what European ethnology is was brought to the centre of attention by the officials in Brussels. As ethnology has been dealing with the territorial *margins* of Europe it is now dealing with *central* political issues! This is a paradox that needs some elaboration. What has become a politically correct issue is that rare virtual reality called 'traditional cultures.' Since the 1970's, the discipline has been shaken to its core by different impulses and critiques of reifying the concept of culture. The traditional field that has for decades been identified as 'European ethnology' has been holding on to the very same definitions.

To study 'European' issues was, until recently, to concentrate on the European *periphery* – in geographical terms, in altitude – high up in mountain regions especially – or far away from the centre. I came to know it intimately when taking my exams some decades ago. European ethnology harboured a proficiency in the subject of sheep in Balkan hills, transhumance in the Alpine regions, the hunting of birds on the North Atlantic coasts, production of cheese where no-one would have believed it was possible, with the aid of age-old implements still surprisingly in use. It was a strange field that seemed untouched by the ongoing debates in the discipline as such – and far removed from the cultural transformation in contemporary Europe. Today this world – where the legacy of ethnology as the discipline dealing with rural culture in different kinds of peripheries – has become possible to use in the construction of European regions. Not only by politicians, but also by people looking for cultural traits that will be rewarding to turn into significant differences.

At the same time – and this is what makes the problem really intriguing – it is looked upon with growing dismay by ethnologists as a kind of simulation of a reality that threatens to overtake the real. The only ethnological professional competence that is being fostered here is that of cultural criticism. That of course is due to the field being old fashioned, but also, to a less obvious extent, to the fact that the very term 'European' has become problematic.

Localising culture and criticising the local.

For the last 30 years, the most innovating studies at different Ethnological Departments all over Europe have been carried out on the *national* situation. Here almost all the big issues have been tried out: the many studies of society and social structure in the 1970's, systems of culture and meaning in the 80's, cultural identities in the 90′s, and the reflexive turn. Deconstructing patterns of culture was also done on domestic topics. Ethnology has been growing into a discipline analysing culture on national level. It has become Anthropology *at home* more than the *Ethnology of Europe.*

Out of all the Swedish doctoral dissertations undertaken in the last two decades, only some ten percent have dealt with non-Swedish topics. Even when scholars have dealt with issues of migration, as Tom O'Dell has pointed out (1998), they have done so from the standpoint of integration – how has migration affected Swedish society? In this way *everyday life* – which has been the topic for ethnological research during these years – has been, to use Akhil Gupta's and James Ferguson's words, 'spatialized' (1992), and 'reifying the linkage of culture and bounded space' as also O'Dell points out. This specialisation into a spatialized Swedish culture has 'created a bastion of reassurance in which ethnologists have felt comfortably at home' (1998:27).

At the popular level, this focus on processes within the nation has led to the almost taken-for-granted assumption that Swedishness has 'some sort of moral charge, with implications of inclusion and exclusion to the nation and the rights associated with membership to it' (O'Dell 1998:27).

Of course ethnologists have become uneasy when watching the classical scene of the Sorcerer's Apprentice, with how results are being misinterpreted and made banal. All of a sudden Swedish became a noun instead of an adjective, as the proof that there was something 'typically Swedish'. Hurrying to the rescue of their profession, ethnologists declared that this was only a construction and that it should not be mistaken for the real thing. There are no such things as place-bound identities and national belonging is not founded on essence or material objects.

Place and Material Culture

It would be fair to say that this readiness to deconstruct was a po-litically necessary step to take, but at the same time made us blind to the creativity inherent in the processes. People's place-bound identities should benefit from our curiosity and become a research topic where we examine how they fit into the many-faceted, post-modern world they are experiencing.

The American philosopher Edward Casey has pointed to the overall openness that characterises places. Places, he says with Bachelard's words, are poetic. They are culturally productive in a particular way. 'The primacy of place is not that of *the* place, much less of *this* place or *a* place (not even a very special place) – all these locutions imply place-as-simple-presence – but that of being an event capable of implacing things in many complex manners and to many complex effects' (1997:337). To do that we should turn our attention away from what has happened in the very place, the nar-ration or historical events that have *taken* place there, and instead see the place's capacity of *holding* and letting events evolve. Casey points out that there is a tendency to overlook the simple fact that every action or narration takes place somewhere and that makes places many-faceted.

From the point of view of identity-formation, the sociologists Mike Featherstone and Scott Lash argue that people are searching for something that is stable – and at the same time characterised by flexibility and contingency. Unlike social identities, places are simultaneously giving scope for chance, whilst supplying a concrete palpability (Featherstone & Lash 1999).

Places can add something to identities that makes them different and therefore new and also create a physical space where identities can evolve or happen. By focusing on place you are able to see how action is meeting dreams in an ever-changing practice (Friedman 1995, O'Dell 1998). The prevailing theories of modernity within our discipline of cultural constructivism have – as we saw above – been putting an emphasis on ideology and 'mind'. First of all, people 'think' an identity and then go into it. These identities could be interpreted as different kind of compensations, as yearnings for 'roots' for those who have gone astray, 'cocooning' for those in search of protection. Therefore the scholar could, all too easily, treat them as them as virtual, as simulations, constructed or invented.

Are identities conscious constructions? To what extent are they the result of physical practices in concrete material surroundings? It would be a mistake to look upon the obsession with place, and with the much-criticised heritage from peasant culture, simply as a *compensation* for the worlds we have lost. That would really turn them into ideology. It is rather an exciting field for studying how something old is recirculated and at the same time renewed. Places are arenas for actions, dreams and practices; they are fields where something new is being tried out.

The Poetics of Istrian Landscapes

In 1966, the American author Edward Stillman published a popular guide to the Balkans. He looked at the Istrian landscape through the lens of the Cold War. What was it but an ideological statement in yet another disguise? What he saw surfacing was an instance of socialism and oppression where even the soil and rocks confirmed its non-western identity:

The Balkans begin in Istria, the peninsula jutting into the Adriatic Sea on the border of Italy. There the northern Italian landscape of cypress trees, pink and tawny stucco farmhouses and green fields passes shockingly into a savage caricature of itself. It becomes a contorted landscape of barren limestone hills and desolate upland pastures under a light so hard and a sky so piercingly blue that in the summer the eye is blinded (1966:9).

The many small medieval towns were depicted as 'retaining a vaguely Italian look, but the entrance to a world of the tragic.'

> Here is an area cut off from the West, not so much by distance as by time, a place where the miseries and crimes of the past live on and are a palpable burden… Great, white lonely peaks, barren of soil or any green, slag and boulders strewn about like the bones of monumental antediluvian beasts. Here for centuries in the pock-marked stone valleys the peasants have grubbed for a bitter livelihood, scooping the life-giving soil from narrow fissures in the rock, carrying it by basket-load to their little walled fields, measuring out their existence in the tiny farms they have cleared in the wastes and tending the gnarled olive trees whose fruit is their only luxury (1966:9,10).

In the 1990's, parallel to the growth of Istria as an officially multicultural region, a stream of books was released. These presentations have one thing in common – trying to free the region from ideology and opening it up to poetic interpretations. In particular, the enigmatic interior with its undulating landscape, numerous hilltops and breathtaking views, has been described in titles that serve well to fire the imagination, such as *Terra Magica, Istria Between Reality and Fiction* (Bertosa 1993), *Terra Incognita* (Fučić 1997), and *Bewitching Istria* (Latković & Dokmanović 1994).[3] In a short space of time the word 'ambient' has begun to appear on the pages of tourist brochures and become a frequently used adjective to show the atmosphere and life of the landscape, its towns and architecture. Istria is now being recognised for its beauty. It is regarded from the same perspective that Loredana Debeljuh and Milani Kruljac were talking about – one associated with the promise of personal reward – the exploration of the self. It must be freed from assumed definitions in order to be the landing ground for fantasies and new practices. To reach to 'its heart of hearts' it has to be freed from the many ideologies and facades that have been covering it. In one of his books from the 1990's, the poet Roman Latković tells how he sets off from nearby Rijeka in search of the elusive spirit of Istria. How during his trip through the landscape he tries with his pen to 'reach the heart of Istria' and how he 'constantly sends her love letters, tests the possibility of depicting the peninsula with a feeling that is ever new'. He 'worships her like a lover. Enraptured time and again by her slightest tremor' (1994:80). And the truth can be found in Istria's independent existence outside time and ideology. It is by coming into personal contact with places and material culture that the answers are to be found.

'This Assertion country, this Croatian country, has been devastated by primitivism, communism, state banditism, careerism, of spiritual dwarfs and by all the other "isms" one can imagine and be disgusted with, and that spiritual vacuum, ugliness and debasement should be subjected to the resistance of the desire for something better, more beautiful' (Latković & Dokmanović 1994:82).

He reaches out to this heart, recovers this spirit when visiting castles, villages, the small towns perched on mountain tops; it lives in wells and in the peculiar white cattle, *boškarin*; in the wine and in the local dishes. This Assertion spirit or *genius loci* is as elusive as it is ever present. It is in the place but it does not offer itself willingly. 'In Grožnjan everything seems to be just here, just around the corner, hidden in the glass of wine of the "Al violina", right here, quite near to you but when you aggressively look around with a desire to grasp its illusive spirit, it vanishes … diabolically keeps out of your reach and disappears, right there, right around the corner. That's Grožnjan. And that is Istria. Everything that is just around the corner, just a few metres away from the main road, and calls for a bit of effort on your part' (Latković & Dokmanović 1994:42).

Such a cult of the landscape for transcendence is always better adapted to the well-to-do middle class and intellectuals. They could use Assertion symbols in a gentrification of themselves. They are also the ones taking the best out of multiculturalism and tolerance. Nevertheless, that would reduce obsession with place to a socially propelled activity. As in the example of Sveti Petar, we could notice how ordinary villagers were clinging to place as that only reliable source of identification in a politically turbulent world. The process of placing culture and tradition by necessity implies a heightened observation of landscape, material culture and nature. This has been possible to articulate in a time when regionalism is in dire need of seeking the local specificity and making the foundation of political sovereignty.

On the level of popular culture, this fascination with landscape and material culture seems to thrive. Last year, at the Ethnographic Museum of Istria in Pazin, an exhibition was showing how ethnographic objects had flooded Istria in the last few years (Škrbić 2001). In July 2001 this exhibition was shown at the Ethnographic Museum in Zagreb.[4] There was an unprecedented market for souvenirs referring to a peasant culture and ancient past, to the landscape itself and its vernacular architecture and monuments. The surprising thing was not the presence of the many souvenirs in this touristified region but the fact that the majority of the products were aimed for the 'home market' and not for tourists. Istria was 'colonising' itself with representations of its landscape and material culture.

When Places Happen

Istria in the 90's gives a picture of how places and material culture become poetic and 'happen' and how this is something rather different from what could be collected under the umbrella of micro-nationalism. A poetic analysis points to how objects could be interpreted when freed from already given definitions, how they could work on the imagination, by *not* being seen as a metaphor, symbolising something else (like 'communism' or 'provincialism'). It is the freeing of dreams, not writing them into any programme: 'I propose, on the contrary, to consider the imagination as a major power of human nature ... By the swiftness of its actions, the imagination separates us from the past as well as from reality; it faces the future.' (Bachelard 1994:xxxiv). According to Bachelard, setting the imagination free runs parallel to anticipating multitude, change and future.

Istria then could be compared to the famous Bachelardian houses. They are not cocooning symbols used for keeping the world out or objects ready to assume our definitions. Instead they are actively made into subjects, transmitters of memories, actors with discrimination and the power to speak and seduce (c.f. Lash 1999:342). A house has the ability to do something to us, just as much as we do things to it. Its most distinctive characteristic is not just that it encloses us and gives us shelter and rest, but that it makes the world open up. It actually functions as a sensory organ through which we investigate life. There is scarcely an idea about the world that is not mediated through open and closed windows or doors, by protective roofs and cosily furnished rooms. Every house is a possibility; it can be the start of a new voyage of discovery. It invites us to take a journey where we can see one dream house after another rolling in front of our eyes – to be examined, approved, or rejected.

When viewed in this way, the redefinition of any European region becomes a place from which dreaming can derive nourishment; it has the ability to contain secrets as well as stepping stones for transcendence. What stories does it give concrete shape to, what associations does it arouse with other regions in other places (cf. Stewart 1996b: 181)? Failing to see the life that proceeds from this new attention given to material culture and places in the regions would be like looking at sheet music but not listening to the music it denotes.

A more varied Istria always appears, because it speaks to your imagination rather than through history. Material culture has become a concrete entry to a complex past. These poetic descriptions portray an Istria that is something to believe in, an entity whose potential is still not fully disclosed but will be realised one day. Thus it takes on the utopian potential of a God, Kaiser Franz Joseph, Mussolini, Tito, the Party or the Nation.[5] Indeed, that was the message of Nelida Milani Kruljac's puzzling utterance when she believed in the power that the territory itself was radiating.

*

As has been repeatedly mentioned in this paper, the many distancing interpretations of the new place-bound regional identities in Europe seem to be a concern coming from Academia as well as from the political viewpoint. What seems necessary to shed light upon today then, is how to approach the matter of local identities from a point of view that puts an emphasis on practice, experience and dreams. It is not that ideology, history or other cultural constructions should be forgotten or overlooked. I think that these have been taken care of. In today's theorising about regional identity it is almost taken for granted that local identity should be understood as some kind of reaction or compensation for some fundamental losses. Within the frame of theories of modernity, any self or collective identity is actively *made*. That is all to the good, but perhaps they are regarded as an answer to the potent dissolving forces in society. 'Glocalisation' is preferably looked upon as a defensive turn against the homogenising forces of globalisation. I have tried to point out some of the difficulties involved in trying to overcome what is habitual in some of the ways we think about regions today. I have tried to show some of the obstacles when it comes to 'un-forgetting', and 'dis-remembering' the many taken-for-granted assumptions about how identities should and could be interpreted as historical constructs and outcomes of ideology.

Focusing on poetics means turning towards a phenomenologically inspired theoretical approach. By the same token it means putting the rather dominating perspectives of modernity and cultural constructionism from the last decade into perspective.

Notes

1   This project is discussed in Hansen, Kjell & Karin Salomonsson 2001. The Departments of European Ethnology at the Universities of Lund in Sweden; Bergen in Norway; Humbolt in Berlin, Germany; Vienna, Austria; Ljubljana, Slovenia; Zagreb, Croatia, and Warsaw, Poland.

2   See 'Articulating Europe. The Mobilisation of Cultural Heritage' Application to EU Commission, Fifth Frame Programme, 2000.

3   In 1997 the cultural historian Branko Fučić published the work Terra incognita, which in a short time has become a standard source for the cultural history of Istria. The historian Miroslav Bertoša, who is a leading authority on the history of the region, refers to the rich occurrence of fictions in his Istra između zbilje

i fikcije ('Istria between Reality and Fiction') from 1993. Terra magica has set the pattern for the presentation of Istria, and the book has been translated into English, German, and Italian.

4   The exhibition was making the periphery present in the Centre, the Capitol. Since Istria is promoting its 'Europeaness' this was not unproblematic in a newly formed country searching for its national identity. With the presence of Istrian musicians, local wine and food the opening turned out to be presenting yet another province of the country – instead of discussing the process of a regionalisation that would bring it closer to neighbouring Slovenia, Italy and Europe .

5   This is supposedly the content of Edward Casey's provocative statement that 'Particular places have taken the place of God and the gods: this is precisely what makes them divine' (1997:341). Place is no longer a location where God or the gods can manifest themselves, while remaining empty while he - or they - are not there. Instead places contain the meaning also deprived of narration, belief or ritual. They have the power to 'generate novel spaces' (op cit).

References

Appadurai, Arjun 1996: *Modernity at Large: Cultural Dimensions of Globalization.* Minneapolis: University of Minnesota Press.

Bachelard, Gaston 1992:. *Jorden och drömmerier om vila.* Lund: Skarabé.

Bachelard, Gaston 1964/94: *The Poetics of Space.* Boston: Beacon Press.

Ballinger, Pamela 1999: Symbolic Boundary Construction at the Borders of the Balkans. http://www.cas.umn.edu/webpapers/ballinge.htm

Beck, Ulrich 1996: *Risk Society. Towards a New Modernity.* London: Sage.

Bertoša, Miroslav 1993: *Istra izmedu zbilje i fikcije.* Zagreb: Matica hrvatska.

Brumen, Borut 2001: Imagined Tradition at the New State Borders. *Proceeedings of the SIEF Conference in Budapest.*

Casey, Edward 1996: How to Get From Space to Place in a Fairly Short Stretch of Time: Phenomenological Prolegomena. In Steven Feld & Keith H. Basso (eds): *Senses of Place.* Santa Fe: School of American Research Press.

Casey, Edward 1998: *The Fate of Place: A Philosophical History.* Berkeley: University of California Press.

Crang, Mike 1998: Place or Space? In: Bell, David & Stephen Wynn Williams (eds)*: Cultural Geography. Routledge Contemporary Human Geography Series.* London.

Featherstone, Mike & Scott Lash (eds) 1999: *Spaces of Culture: City – Nation – World.* London: Sage

Friedman, Jonathan 1995: Global System, Globalization and the Parameters of Modernity. In: Featherstone, Mike & Scott Lash, R, Robertson (eds): *Global Modernities*, pp: 69–90. London: Sage.

Frykman, Jonas 2001: Belonging in Europe. Modern Identities in Minds and Places. Niedermüller, Peter & Bjarne Stoklund (eds) *Europe. Cultural Construction and Reality.* Museum Tusculanum Press. University of Copenhagen. pp: 13–24.

Frykman, Jonas 1999: National Identities: Between Modernity and Cultural Nationalism. In *Volkskultur und Moderne: Europäische Ethnologie zur Jahrtausendwende*. *Festschrift für Konrad Köstlin*. *Europäische Ethnologie 21*. Vienna.

Fučić, Branko 1997: *Terra incognita*. Zagreb: Kršćanska sadašnjost.

Giddens, Anthony 1990: *The Consequences of Modernity*. Cambridge: Polity Press.

Giddens, Anthony 1991: *Modernity and Self-Identity: Self and Society in the Late Modern Age*. Cambridge: Polity Press.

Gupta, Akhil & James Ferguson 1992: Beyond 'Culture': Space, Identity, and the Politics of Difference. *Cultural Anthropology*, Volume 7, Number 1. pp: 6–23.

Kappus, Elke-Nicole 2001: Ethnographischer Blick. In: Istrien: Sichtweisen. *Kittseer Schriften zur Volkskunde. 13*.

Klein, Barbro 2000: 'Folklore, Heritage Politics and Ethnic Diversity': Thinking About the Past and the Future. In: *Folklore, Heritage Politics and Ethnic Diversity A Festschrift for Barbro Klein*. Botkyrka: Mångkulturellt Centrum.

Lash, Scott 1999: *Another Modernity: A Different Rationality*. Oxford: Blackwell.

Latković, Roman & Dokmanović, Ranko. 1994: *Bewitching Istria: A Never Ending Story*. Rijeka: Carli.

Latour, Bruno 1998: *Artefakternas återkomst: Ett möte mellan organisationsteori och tingens sociologi*. Göteborg: Nerenius förlag.

Lowenthal, David 1996: *Possessed by the Past: The Heritage Crusade and the Spoils of History*. New York: The Free Press.

Marcus, George 1992: Past, Present and Emerging Identities. In: Jonathan Friedman & Scott Lash (eds): *Modernity and Identity*. London: Blackwell.

Massey, Doreen 1994: *Space, Place and Gender*. Cambridge: Polity Press.

Melucci, Alberto 1991: *Nomads of the Present: Social Movements and Individual Needs in Contemporary Society*. Philadelphia: Temple.

Morley, David & Robins, Kevin 1995: No Place like Heimat: Images of Home(land). In: Morley, David & Kevin Robin (eds): *Spaces of Identity. Global Media, Electronic Landscapes and Cultural Boundaries*. Routledge: London. pp: 85–104.

Nikočević, Lidija & Nevena Škrbić 2001: Österreich-Mythen in Istrien. In: Istrien: Sichtweisen. *Kittseer Schriften zur Volkskunde. 13*.

O'Dell, Tom 1998: Junctures of Swedishness. Reconsidering Representations of the National. *Ethnologia Scandinavica*. pp: 20–37.

Rakovac, Milan 1997: Die 'Istrianizierung' Europas. In *Istrien. Europa erlese*. Frankfurt: Wieser Verlag.

Rakovac, Milan 2001: Europa. In: Istrien: Sichtweisen. *Kittseer Schriften zur Volkskunde. 13*.

Salomonsson, Karin 2001: E-ekonomin och det kulinariska kulturarvet. I: (Hansen, Kjell & Karin Salomonsson (red): *Europa. Platser och identiteter*. Lund: Studentlitteratur.

Shore, Chris 2000: *Building Europe: The Cultural Politics of European Integration*. London: Routledge.

Škrbić, Nevena 2001: Istrien heute 'von Innen'. In: Istrien: Sichtweisen. *Kittseer Schriften zur Volkskunde. 13*.

Stewart, Kathleen 1996a: An Occupied Place. In Steven Feld & Keith H. Basso (eds), *Senses of Place*. Santa Fe: School of American Research Press.

Stewart, Kathleen 1996b: *A Space on the Side of the Road: Cultural Poetics in an 'Other' America.* Princeton: Princeton University Press.

Stillman, Edmund 1966: *The Balkans. Life World Library.* Time-Life International. Nederland. N.V.

Contributors

JONAS FRYKMAN is professor of European Ethnology at Lund University and formerly at the University of Bergen. In a number of books – among them *Culture Builders: A Cultural Anthropology of Middle Class Life* (1987) and *Force of Habit* (1991) – both with Orvar Löfgren, he has been studying culture and modernity in 20th-century Sweden. In books like *Identities in Pain* (1998 – edited with Nadia Seremetakis and Susanne Ewert) he has been writing on body and identity. Central themes in his production are socialisation, masculinity, education and national identity. He is currently working on place and European identities, see *Ethnologia Europaea* 2003, 32:2. Jonas Frykman is the editor of *Ethnologia Scandinavica*.

NILS GILJE is professor at the Department of Cultural Studies and Art History at the University of Bergen. His background is in philosophy, and he has previously been professor of philosophy of science in Bergen. Gilje has published several books in philosophy, among them *History of Western Thought* (1999 – translated into seven languages) and *The Philosophical Presuppositions of the Social Sciences* (1996). He has recently written a book (together with Tarald Rasmussen) on Norwegian intellectual history in the early Modern period: *Intellectual Life in a Lutheran State: A History of Norwegian Ideas 1537–1814* (2002, in Norwegian). Gilje is presently working on magic and witchcraft in post-reformation Norway.

GHASSAN HAGE is associate professor of anthropology at the University of Sydney. He works in the areas of nationalism, racism, multiculturalism and transnational migration. He has been a visiting professor in many international universities including the American University of Beirut, the École des hautes études en Sciences Sociale, Paris, and the University of Copenhagen. His works include *White Nation: Fantasies of White Supremacy in a Multicultural Society* (2000), *Arab-Australians: Citizenship and*

Belonging (2002) and most recently, *Against Paranoid Nationalism: Searching for Hope in a Shrinking Society* (2003). He is currently doing fieldwork on transnational kinship among Lebanese migrants, a multi-sited ethnography which includes London, Paris, Caracas, Philadelphia and Sydney.

KJELL HANSEN is teaching and doing research at the Department of European Ethnology at Lund University. He works in the areas of rural development, regionalism and European Studies. His thesis *Välfärdens motsträviga utkant* (1998) – The Reluctant Margins of Welfare – treated regional identities in inland Northern Sweden as an answer to and opposition against state policies. He has been co-editing *Fönster mot Europa* (2001) – Window towards Europe – and is presently working on a book on the relations between European identification, everyday life, and cultural heritage.

MICHAEL JACKSON is professor in anthropology at the Institute of Anthropology at the University of Copenhagen. The author of numerous works of ethnography, including the award-winning *Paths Toward a Clearing* (1989) and *At Home in the World* (1995), Michael Jackson has also published works of fiction and poetry. He has carried out extensive fieldwork in Aboriginal Australia and Sierra Leone, and has recently completed a book that interweaves an account of Sierra Leone since Independence with episodes from the life of a prominent Sierra Leone politician. He is presently working on a sequel to *Paths Toward a Clearing*.

FRANCINE LORIMER is amanuensis at the Institute of Anthropology, University of Copenhagen. Her Ph.D. fieldwork among Kuku-Yalanji in Cape York is a phenomenological account of experiences of country and personhood among Aboriginal people in a context of radical social change. Lorimer has also reviewed psychiatric studies of Aboriginal society and written reports for the Central Land Council and the Cape York Land Council on social change and local history. She is currently writing on the notion of knowledge in anthropological research and writing.

KIRSTI MATHIESEN HJEMDAHL has a PhD in ethnology from the Department of Cultural Studies and Art History, University of Bergen. She has been working on tourism and pedagogy. Hjemdahl's thesis *Tur/retur temapark* (Return Ticket to the Theme Park) (2003) is based on the analysis of theme parks, which focuses both on the consumption and production. Several papers are available in English. These are available on line, at her website: www.kulturviter.no. She is presently engaged in comparative fieldwork on the politics of place in Croatia and South Africa.

MAJA POVRZANOVIĆ FRYKMAN is a Research fellow in ethnology at the Department of International Migration and Ethnic Relations, Malmö University, and an external associate of Institute of Ethnology and Folklore Research in Zagreb. She has published on experiences and representations of war and exile, as well as on concepts and practices within the semantic domains of diaspora and transnationalism. She co-edited *War, Exile, Everyday Life: Cultural Perspectives* (1996), and edited *Beyond Integration: Challenges of Belonging in Diaspora and Exile* (2001).